The Military Career of General Lew Wallace: Mexico to Monocacy

David B. McCoy

The Military Career of General Lew Wallace: Mexico to Monocacy © 2018 David B. McCoy

ISBN: 9781983011016

Spare Change Press®
Est. 1979

Short non-fiction, history-related publications.

sparechangepress.weebly.com

amazon.com/author/davidmccoy

Royalties (after expenses) are donated to non-profit organizations.

sparechangepress79@gmail.com

I would like to thank Mary Ann D'Aurelio and Dr. Rhonda Baughman for proofreading.

Also, I wish to thank the following who helped with image permissions, research, and content advice:

- Jodie Steelman Wilson, MLS, Assistant Director, Crawfordsville District Public Library
- Michael Ellis, Head of Access Services, Reference, and Interlibrary Loan Duggan Library, Hanover College
- Christelle Venham, Reference Specialist and Library Associate West Virginia University
- Ann Harvey, Assistant Director, Montgomery County Historical Society of Indiana
- Larry Paarlberg, and all the staff, of the General Lew Wallace Study & Museum
- Roger Cain of Colfax, Indiana

Map illustrations for battles mentioned in this book can be found at:

http://portfolio.shep.design/map-illustrations-for-shadow-of-shiloh-book

To enlarge a map, click on it three times.

*   *   *

INTRODUCTION

The introduction for this publication is being written a few miles north of Antietam National Battlefield, Sharpsburg, Maryland. It was here while volunteering for the park service's spring cleanup via Roads Scholar I first learned of the Battle of Monocacy.

Several years ago, while waiting for the evening speaker to arrive, I perused the books about the Battle of Antietam left out for our enjoyment by the staff of the facility where we were housed. One book that truly caught my attention was Franklin B. Cooling's *Monocacy: The Battle That Saved Washington*. I assure you, I am no Civil War scholar, but I did spend most of my career teaching American History through Reconstruction and had never heard of the Battle of Monocacy. I became even more intrigued when I learned, first, the battlefield is only 30 miles east of Antietam, and second, it was the site where in 1862 a member of Lee's staff lost Special Order 191 leading to the Battle of Antietam.

Special Order 191 display, Best Farm, Monocacy Battlefield

Not being one to rush into any writing topic, I casually began reading books mostly about Lew Wallace who is credited with winning the battle. (Oddly, winning the battle in this case meant delaying the Confederate force moving towards Washington D.C. long enough for Union reinforcements to arrive.) As I have come to believe, anyone who reads anything relating to Lew Wallace is captivated by his personality. Just some of the words used to describe him include: impatient, arrogant, self-serving.

Consequently, over time, the focus of the intended book changed from one being about the Battle of Monocacy to the military career of Lew Wallace from Mexico to Monocacy. While that was an easy change to make, Wallace's seemingly larger than life personality caused me problems. It easily could have overtaken my intent, so I consciously minimized it. Instead, I decided to set my sights on more meaningful topics—Wallace's military career, the struggle at the time between volunteer and regular army generals, his evolving views on slavery and emancipation, and the continued controversy of his first day's march at the Battle of Shiloh in 1862.

The second major decision I had to make was in relation to Wallace's writing career. As many readers may know, Wallace wrote *Ben-Hur: A Tale of the Christ*, which became a best seller by the beginning of the 20th century (and remained so until the publication of *Gone with the Wind*). It would also be made into three movies, the most recent being in 2016. Instead of discussing his writing career, I decided it would be more interesting to include passages from his *An Autobiography* pertinent to the various topics covered.

By the turn of the 20th century, Wallace was focusing his efforts on the writing of his *An Autobiography*. However, at the time of his death on February 15, 1905, forty years of his life remained unrecorded. Wallace's widow, Susan, with the assistance of friend and author, Mary Hannah Krout, completed the autobiography using correspondence and articles written by Lew Wallace.

Ironically, when he put his pen down for the final time, it is reported he had just completed his memories of the Battle of Monocacy.

CHAPTER 1: *Militias*

Lew Wallace was born into a prominent Indiana political family on April 10, 1827. His grandfather, Andrew Wallace, was a close friend of William Henry Harrison and served with him during the War of 1812. (Harrison was also the hero of the Battle of Tippecanoe and later elected in 1841 as the ninth President of the United States.) Through Harrison, Andrew secured an appointment to West Point for Lew's father, David. Upon his return to Indiana, David served as lieutenant-governor (1831-1837), governor (1838-1840), and as a one-term U.S. congressman for Indiana (1841-1843). His maternal grandfather, John Test, served two terms as a U.S. congress-man for Indiana and later was presiding judge of the Indiana Circuit Court.

Lew's namesake was "Major" Samuel Lewis, who was 3 years older than David Wallace and courted David's sister Catherine. Samuel and Catherine were married on December 10, 1818. Samuel was elected to the Indiana General Assembly in 1826. There is some mystery as to why he was identified as Major Samuel Lewis. He was too young for the War of 1812. Probably he was associated with a local militia unit at Brookville, Indiana.

Perhaps Lew's most important political connection was with his boyhood friend, Oliver Morton. Both had attended Wayne County Seminary (later renamed Whitewater College) with Morton going on to become Indiana's "Civil War" governor. It would be Morton who appointed Lew Adjutant-General of Indiana in 1861 and commissioned him Colonel of the 11th Indiana Volunteer Infantry.

*   *   *

When Lew was five years old, David moved the family to Covington, Indiana, near the Illinois frontier. Shortly after arriving at their new home, Native Americans under Chief Black Hawk killed two settlers in Illinois. In an 1804 treaty, the Sauk and Fox tribes had ceded their lands in Illinois and in 1828 relocated west of the Mississippi. Black Hawk and other tribal members disputed the treaty, claiming the leaders who signed the treaty had done so without full tribal authorization. In 1832, Chief Black Hawk led a band of Sauk and Fox against American settlers in Illinois and present-day Wisconsin in what would become known as the Black Hawk War.

In response to fears that Black Hawk would turn his followers against the small settlement, David Wallace—no doubt the one Covington resident with the most military background—organized and drilled a company of men as a precaution. Their display of military vigilance so impressed young Lew, he soon dreamed of becoming a soldier and marching off to war behind the nation's flag. In his 1906 *An Autobiography*, Wallace wrote:

Early one morning … The public square, when I reached it after breakfast, was fast filling with people from the out-towns and country, and I had only to look at their attire to know that something warlike was at hand. It will not do for me to say they were in uniform. Their coats were bedizened with cotton cords and tape in various forms and hues … A few swords were in Place … Sometimes I shuddered to see a musket; though, as a rule, the

martial apparitions were armed with umbrellas,
corn-stalks, and hickory staves. The sky above
them seemed tremulous with the thunder of
bass-drums.

After dinner a cavalcade in diverse uniforms,
some with immense hats half-moon in form and
gorgeously plumed, trotted to our gate. My
father went out to them, himself in blue
frock-coat, brass buttons, sash, and hat of
the same half-moon style, mounted with a white
silk cockade.

Afar off I saw the crowd form and march away
in leading of the big-hatted horsemen and the
thunderous drums. They took the road to the
river-bottom, and over their heads in the
going I saw for the first time the flutter and
stream of colors, or, more simply, the flag
which was to become better known to me as "Old
Glory."

In a razzle-dazzle … I stole down to a secure
ambush of ironweeds on the hill-side and
watched the militia of the county in
regimental drill, Colonel (Lieutenant-
Governor) Wallace commanding. They would wheel
into column — and ploy and deploy, and change
front [in spite of] the canes, corn-stalks, .
and umbrellas … I do not hesitate to say that
to the dazed reviewer in the ironweeds on the
hill-side, nothing of military circumstances
half so splendid and inspiring had ever taken
place.

When night came, and my mother tucked me in
the little trundle-bed with my elder brother,
I had gained such store of wisdom pertaining
to war that it passed into my dreams, and from
them into my life.

* * *

In the 1837 election, David Wallace was elected Governor of Indiana and moved his family to Indianapolis. There, the ten-year-old Lew discovered Indianapolis was the home of a successful military militia company called the City Greys. Most of its members were wealthier, older, and more established citizens of Indianapolis who were able to equip themselves with excellent uniforms, up-to-date muskets and bayonets, and even a brass band.

Its success led Lew to join the newly formed Marion Rifles, where he "had the honor to be elected second sergeant" (*An Autobiography*, 1906). Unlike the Greys, the ranks of the Rifles were filled with young men—mostly incapable of mustaches—dressed in caps and cotton hunting-shirts fashioned after General Daniel Morgan's of Revolutionary Riflemen. The Greys marched to the sonorous music of a brass-band while the Rifles were content with a fife and drum.

As noted by Wallace, "The differences between the companies were not of a kind to foster what the French call camaraderie." The Rifles despised the aristocratic airs of the Greys, while the Greys insulted the Rifles by calling them "Arabs." The Rifles got revenge for the name calling during a mock battle cele-brating the anniversary of Andrew Jackson's victory over the British at the Battle of New Orleans in 1812. In Wallace's words, here is how the display unfolded and the impact it would have on the sixteen-year-old (*An Autobiography*, 1906):

We were posted at the intersection of Meridian Street, facing eastward; while, turning from Delaware up by the court-house, the [Greys] moved to the attack in a column of sections, their band playing vociferously. Their appearance was beautiful … The Greys opened with volleys; we replied, lying down and firing at will. All went well until in the crisis of the engagement our captain forgot to order [our prearranged] retreat … The mêlée that ensued was tremendous. [Paper] wads [from our muskets] flew like bullets. We shot one man, took several prisoners, and were, left masters of the field. At sight of the haughty foe in flight I yelled my throat into tatters. The incident is, of course, trivial; yet it was of consequence to me. It put a final finish upon the taste for military life by turning it into a genuine passion. It was my initiation into the Ancient and Honorable Order of Soldiers.

About this same time, a volume of Winfield Scott's *Infantry Tactics: Or Rules For The Exercise And Maneuvers Of The United States' Infantry* fell into Lew's hands which further stimulated his interest in commanding troops and tactics. He believed intense study of this work might make him a "drill-master," and spent much of his time discussing the book and various tactical drills with the Rifle's company captain. Such study would prove to be a good preparation for a future colonel of infantry, but not for the lawyer David Wallace hoped his son would become.

CHAPTER 2

PART ONE
OVERVIEW OF THE MEXICAN AMERICAN WAR*

The Mexican American War or the (U.S.-Mexico War) was a war fought between the United States and Mexico between 1846 and 1848.

In 1835, Texas battled and gained independence from Mexico, becoming a sovereign country for the next decade. In the Treaty of Velasco granting independence, the Texas-Mexico border was established along the Rio Grande. Mexican President Antonio Lopez de Santa Anna (pronounced "Santana") signed the treaty, but the Mexican Congress never ratified it, nor did Mexican presidents after Santa Anna acknowledge Texas' independence.

Texas was annexed by the United States in 1845. Mexico claimed the international border to be the Nueces River, while the U.S. claimed the border to be at the Rio Grande. On assuming the American presidency in 1845, James K. Polk attempted to secure the boundary at the Rio Grande and to the sale of northern California. (Polk had adopted an aggressive policy to ensure the completion of "Manifest Destiny". This was the belief that the United States had a God-given right to eventually control the entire continent. Americans migrating to the West thought they could manage the land better than Native American nations or the Mexican government.) What Polk failed to realize was that pressure would not work because Mexican politicians could not yield of any territory, including Texas.

Frustrated by the Mexican refusal to negotiate, Polk, on January 13, 1846, directed General Zachary Taylor's army at Corpus Christi to advance to the Rio Grande. (Because Taylor was a man who preferred a simple appearance, many soldiers felt he looked more like a farmer than a general in his straw hat and linen duster.) The Mexican government viewed this as an act of war. On April 25, the Mexican troops at Matamoros crossed the river and ambushed an American patrol. Polk seized upon the incident to secure a declaration of war on May 13 on the basis of the shedding of "American blood upon American soil." Meanwhile, on May 8 and 9, Taylor's 2,200-man army defeated 3,700 Mexicans under General Mariano Arista in the battles of Palo Alto and Resaca de la Palma.

The U.S. army fought its way overland into Mexico from California, Texas, and eventually from Veracruz straight to the capital. Mexico's Santa Anna, back in power, sent a peace treaty to Washington in early 1847, but his terms were not acceptable. Later that year, with U.S. troops just outside Mexico City, peace talks occurred. When Mexico would not admit defeat and offer up territory, American troops invaded the capital city and quickly took control. Santa Anna resigned as president and fled central Mexico in defeat. The United States now occupied the Mexican capital.

President Polk sent "Peace Ambassador" Nicholas Trist to central Mexico to set the terms of the treaty. With the Treaty of Guadalupe-Hidalgo of February 2, 1848, the American Southwest as we know it today (New Mexico, Colorado, Utah, Nevada, Arizona and most of California) officially came under U.S. control with Mexico losing half of its country. The treaty established the Texas-Mexican border along the Rio Grande but permitted a group of surveyors from each country, working together, to map the new 2,000-mile long border.

PART TWO

*Word came up from Texas that General Taylor had
razed his beautiful camp on the Nueces Bay, and,
with a force enlarged to the proportions of a respectable
army, was in full march for the Rio Grande River.*

*That there would be war was no longer doubtful.
The Mexicans were in force waiting ...
I was to have my wish.
There would be a battle, then other battles. Hurrah!*

—Lew Wallace

When Congress declared war on Mexico on May 13, 1846, the
federal government called upon Indiana to provide enough
troops for three regiments (each comprising of ten
companies). When this call went out, Indiana had no
organized militia and no military equipment worthy of notice.
Before its admission as a state, the militia of Indiana had been
kept in excellent condition, but with the passing of the War of
1812 and of Indian troubles, interest in military affairs waned.
Furthermore, the adjutant-general was a mere title holder,
usually ignorant of the requirements of his office. While poorly
equipped in the materials for making war, when the call for
regiments went out, Indiana was fortunate in having David
Reynolds as Adjutant-General. While he knew nothing
concerning military operations, he was intelligent and willing
to learn. Furthermore, he possessed courage, some executive
ability, common sense, and was a tireless worker.

Under David Reynolds recruiting began in earnest. While the
state had no organized militia, there were a few remaining
independent militias, but from a "military" perspective, they

were "a joke" (R. C. Buley, *Indiana Magazine of History*, 1919). Even so, many of the "cornstalk" militia enrolled in total. Scores of young men took it upon themselves to raise companies, hoping to be rewarded for their trouble with a commissioned rank. One of these young men who raised a company was Lew Wallace. As Wallace wrote in his *An Autobiography*:

I found Adjutant-General Reynolds in a mood communicative. The mail of the day preceding had brought the governor an official notice that Congress, besides formally declaring war against Mexico, had appropriated ten million dollars to carry it on, and authorized the president to call out fifty thousand volunteers.

This was great news, and I made haste to ask: "Will any of the troops be from Indiana?" "Yes, that's what's bothering me," the general replied. " We are asked to furnish three regiments — and the business is entirely new — no forms, no precedents — nothing for our guidance."

I was shaking with excitement.
"Well," I asked, "can anyone raise a company? Or must authority be first had from the governor?" "I suppose any one can go about it; only when raised it must, of course, be tendered to the governor for regimental assignment and muster-in." I went out resolved to raise a company, if no one older and better known did not set about it.

Renting a room on Washington Street in the center of Indianapolis, Wallace hired a drummer and a fifer to attract attention. He also hung a flag and a four-sided transparency, inscribed FOR MEXICO, FALL IN. Within three days, he had recruited enough men for a company.

An example of a four-sided transparency

A company consisted of one captain, one first-lieutenant, one second-lieutenant, four sergeants, four corporals, two musicians and eighty privates (men). The commissioned officers of each company were elected after the company was full by a majority of the members. Nineteen-year-old Wallace was elected second-lieutenant of Company H, 1st Indiana Volunteer Infantry.

Upon receiving their orders, the three regiments first traveled to the Falls of the Ohio. (Today, the Falls of the Ohio is a state park in Indiana. It is located on the banks of the Ohio River at Clarksville, Indiana, across from Louisville, Kentucky. The Falls of the Ohio was never a classic waterfall such as Niagara Falls or even Cumberland Falls in Kentucky. It has been described as a series of rapids that drop the river level about 26 feet over a length of about two and a half miles. This is the only place in the nearly thousand-mile length of the Ohio River that posed a major navigation obstacle. The Falls was the site where, in 1804, Meriwether Lewis met William Clark for the Corps of Discovery Expedition.) There the regiments were assembled, organized, equipped, and mustered into the national service, and remained at "Camp Clark" two weeks. On July 5th they boarded steamboats chartered to transport them to New Orleans.

Landing below the city, the volunteers awaited the arrival of sailing ships to carry them across the gulf. Here the men were introduced to the soldier's life without the frills. Through mismanagement of the officers, the troops were compelled to pitch their tents on a stretch of blubbery slime. There, straw and brush were unattainable, and the ooze went through the army blanket much as water goes through a sieve. At first, Wallace found the conditions deplorable, but soon turned his attention elsewhere.

Wallace:

Along with the rest, I was wretched until an old negro peddling eggs and chickens visited us. He told me casually that we were occupying a portion of the field Andrew Jackson turned into a garden of [victory] in 1815. Then I

hired him as a guide. The battle-ground was
more interesting to me than the city. Where
was the breastwork of cotton? Where did
Jackson's line begin on the right? In what
direction did it stretch? That line fixed, I
had the key to the fight; standing on it, I
faced the British assaults, and in the
patriotic indulgence of fancy cared not a whit
whether I was on a slippery tussock or knee -
deep in water. Four killed here; two red-
coated thousands yonder!

Three ships at last arrived on July 17 and 18. Then, once
getting their moldy goods stowed, the 1st Indiana sailed for
Brazos de Santiago, on the other side of the gulf.

———

* Overview of the Mexican American War adapted from:

Mexican American War and the Treaty of Guadalupe-Hidalgo
https://www.nps.gov/cham/learn/historyculture/mexican-
american-war.htm

Mexican American War History
http://www.thomaslegion.net/mexicanwar.html

CHAPTER 3: *Mexico*

About sunset, July 26, 1846, the ships bearing the Indiana volunteers reached Brazos island. The island was a waste of sand dunes about three and one-half miles wide. The soil was bare, there was no grass, not even a tree. A solitary hut, half buried by sand, was the only dwelling in sight.

There were close to five thousand troops camped at Brazos. Diarrhea and measles quickly took its toll on the men. The water was blamed for the diarrhea, but it is more likely the food was the main culprit. Also, the wind which swept over the island blew sand into the soldiers' food, eyes, and ears.
On July 30, the 1st and 3rd Indiana Volunteer Regiments left for the mouth of the Rio Grande, eight miles down the beach from Brazos. Four days later, they arrived at the new encampment named Camp Belknap. Conditions there were even worse than at Brazos. The camp was a mile from the river, and the men were forced to wade through a swamp to get water.

Upon arrival, the 1st Indiana expected to remain there a few weeks before receiving marching orders to take part in the Monterrey Campaign. To their surprise, though, General Taylor ordered them to remain behind to guard his lines of communication. Then in late August, a second order from Taylor sent the regiment into an unnamed garrison at the mouth of the Rio Grande. Across the river, a ragged Mexican hamlet, nick-named "Bagdad," harbored a band of smugglers. This time, the move was to guard a steamboat landing.
It did not take long for Wallace to question the wisdom of Taylor's orders.

Wallace:

A monotony descended upon the camp — a monotony unrelieved as an arctic night … Now and
then we heard of operations by General Taylor.
A steamboat man would stray in among us with
the news. General Taylor had set out from
Matamoras for the up-country; then had taken
Camargo, the enemy having abandoned it; and
thereafter, with a regiment in garrison at
Matamoras, there was not the slightest need of
us where we were — none earthly. A post-guard
of twenty men would have been ample to hold
the mouth of the Rio Grande.

How the scourge got into our camp, whether by
the river, or by the spoiled pork we ate,
calling it meat, or by the bad cookery which
was the rule with the messes, or by all these
causes in combination … The soldier may have
been in perfect health the day we went into
the camp, [but after] three weeks having
passed, I notice a change in his appearance.
His cheeks have the tinge of old gunny-sacks;
under the jaws the skin is ween and flabby;
his eyes are filmy and sinking; he moves
listlessly … Another week and his place in the
ranks is vacant. A messmate answers for him.
No need of looking for him in the hospital.

By the end of October 1846, after two months at the mouth of
the Rio Grande, sixty-three members of the 1st Indiana were
dead from various diseases. This would be a turning point in
Wallace's view of Taylor, West Point officers, and in how

volunteers—despite leaving their homes, families, and livelihoods—were left behind while army regulars did all the fighting and gained all the glory.

*   *   *

In September, Taylor had advanced from Camargo to Monterrey which he captured in four days of hard fighting—leaving nearly 20 percent of his men dead. Yet, had he fought one more day, he could have destroyed General Pedro de Ampudia's army. Instead, Taylor let the Mexicans evacuate without pursuit and agreed to an eight-week armistice. While Colonel Stephen Kearny was conquering New Mexico and California during the fall of 1846, Taylor remained immobile at Walnut Springs, his headquarters north of Monterrey. Not until December did he finally move against Santa Anna. It was at this moment, General Robert Patterson—without Taylor's permission or knowledge—ordered the 1st Indiana, first by boat 210 miles up the Rio Grande to Camargo, then overland 180 miles to Walnut Springs on the war front. (Wallace would later learn Patterson "acted from pity, having never seen men in the service in such a state of neglect and suffering.")

As the men neared the end of their march, their feet grew heavy but their hearts were light, for at last they were to become a part of the army. However, when they were within six miles of Walnut Springs, without warning, the 1st Indiana was called to a halt. A courier rode up to Colonel Drake and delivered a dispatch to him. He read it. He read it twice. His face turned much redder than usual. Something had hit him hard, yet he managed to give commands for the men to "faced front," and bring their arms to "order." Colonel Drake tried to read the dispatch, but choked, and handed it to his adjutant to finish. When the adjutant was through they all stood dazed.

Taylor ordered the 1st Indiana, not back to the mouth of the Rio Grande, but to the border town of Matamoros—the first large border town in Mexico captured by the Americans on May 18, 1846.

While descending the Rio Grande to Matamoros, Wallace would see his first and only fighting in the War. It was thought it would only take four days to reach Matamoros, and thus only four days of rations were issued. However, they were scarcely half-way at the end of the fifth day and it became necessary to send five men out in search of cattle. Two men quickly returned to tell how the party had been ambushed and three of their comrades killed. The captain of the boat, Captain Milroy, suspected the villain was General María Jesús Carbajal, a guerrilla leader whose headquarters was the nearby town of Reynosa. The captain called for volunteers to attack the town. Four companies responded, with Wallace commanding the men of Company H. One company was left to guard the steamer.

Wallace:

The dead men were found horribly mutilated.
Tearing through the brush, then, we reached
the town, where, as a glance disclosed, the
advantages were all against us. First, a
stretch of meadow-land; then bluff fifteen or
twenty feet high, its face gullied by rains;
at the edge of the bluff on top a palisade of
tree-trunks set side and side, and taller than
our heads; behind the palisade the enemy — how
many we could not see. I could see their guns
glistening in the sunlight. So, by the signs,
I had stumbled on my first fight, though at

the moment too much excited to recognize the fact.

There was a brief halt while Milroy arranged the attack. Then, in double files, and with a yell, we rushed across the meadow. I was in command of Company H. Heavens! What furnace heat there was in that go! We reached the foot of the bluff, and not a shot had been fired at us. How I got up the face of the bluff I do not know; how over the tall palisading I would never have known had not some of the men afterwards spoken of the boosting they gave me. And then the disappointment! The Mexicans ran out of the town into the chaparral [leaving behind] one killed and four wounded.

The 1st Indiana had hardly settled in their new quarters at Matamoros before orders again came to proceed to Walnut Springs. For the third time, the regiment covered the long route but reached its destination without interruption.

As the men drew near General Taylor's headquarters, they became anxious to see the general in spite of the poor treatment they had received from him. They expected to find a magnificent tent with staff officers wearing flashy uniforms. They found only a flagpole on which flew a dirty flag, a dingy tent, a plain table and a few camp chairs. And of General Taylor himself.

Wallace:

Leaning lazily against the butt of the white pole, I saw a man of low stature, dressed in a blouse unbuttoned and so faded it could not be said to have been of any color, a limp-bosomed shirt certainly not white, a hang-down collar without a tie of any kind, trousers once light blue now stripeless, rough marching shoes, foxy from long wear — such the dress of the man. I did not salute him, but, like all who had preceded me, and all who came after me, pressed on wondering, where can he [General Taylor]be?

It is important to understand, for Wallace, casual dress in a general was unacceptable. The man must look the part—even when conditions or fighting were difficult—in order to inspire the troops.

Another fear Wallace had at this time was that by the time 1st Indiana reached Walnut Springs, the Battle of Buena Vista had already entered the history books. On February 22-23, 1847, Taylor's army of 4,600 had defeated a Mexican arm of more than 15,000. Taylor was not on the field when the Mexicans attacked, but when he arrived, saw the 2nd Indiana fleeing the battle. After the battle, he criticized not only the Second's retreat, but *all* the Hoosier volunteers for cowardice [regardless of the fact, the 1st was not there for the battle]. For Wallace, honor was not an abstract concept, but a very important, tangible part of his identity. It was something he strove throughout his life to obtain and maintain. As a result, he played a leading role in making sure Taylor did not carry Indiana in the 1848 election.

While Wallace experienced little combat in Mexico, he did acquire some understanding of logistics and supply, mentioning that he "went with the companies which escorted the 250 [wagon] train as far as Matamoros ... Each wagon was drawn by five mules, the whole of them together, from front to rear, covered track two miles in length" (Wallace to William "Bill" Wallace, from Camp Rio Grande, October 22,1846, Lew Wallace Collection).

Wallace also gained some experience in dealing with sickness. More than 11,000 of the 116,000 American soldiers who served in Mexico died of disease, while only 1,700 had been battle casualties. As little new understanding of diseases developed until after the Civil War, for every three soldiers killed in battle, five more died of disease.

The Indiana regiment left Mexico for New Orleans on May 24,1847, to be mustered out. Wallace returned to Indianapolis to study law with his father, eventually applying again to take the state bar exam. (Prior to the war, Wallace's father had encouraged his son to study law, but Lew found it to be an arduous task. He did make one attempt at passing the bar but failed, and eagerly directed his attention on the chance for military glory in Mexico.) By the summer of 1851, and again in 1852, he was elected as the prosecuting attorney of Indiana's Eighth Judicial Circuit. Despite being a fairly successful prosecutor, he found riding the circuit dull with drab accommodations and little in the way of entertainment. For Wallace, the law was only a way to earn a living, and later in life he referred to it as the "most detestable of human occupations."

In April 1853, Wallace resigned his job as prosecuting attorney in Covington, Indiana, and moved to Crawfordsville, where he set himself up in private practice. Besides there being more money in private practice, by this time he was married to Susan Elston, the daughter of Isaac Compton Elston, a wealthy

Crawfordsville merchant and land speculator. Furthermore, Wallace and Susan had a young son, and a small piece of land, given to them by Susan's father, to build a home.

As before, he proved to be a successful lawyer, but his passions during the 1850s were politics and the military unit he established.

CHAPTER 4: *Politics*

During the 1850s, tensions over the issue of slavery spread to the western territories and the nation seemed to be on a course toward disunion. After 1854, when open warfare broke out in the Kansas Territory among slaveholders, abolitionists, and opportunists, the battle lines of opinion hardened rapidly. President Buchanan quieted Kansas by calling in the Regular Army, but it was too small and too scattered to suppress the fighting that continued until 1861, when Kansas became a state.

*   *   *

Foreseeing war as the result of the fighting in Kansas and the fragmented citizenry, Wallace sought and received a commission as captain and the authority to create Montgomery Guard Independent Militia from the governor in May 1856. The Guards had sixty muskets, drilled three nights a week, and at first wore the U.S. Regulars' uniforms. Then after reading about the colorful uniforms and fearless fighting tactics used by the Zouaves, a French unit from Algeria in North Africa, the Montgomery Guard adopted both Zouave drill and uniforms. A light infantry unit, the Zouaves moved rapidly and athletically, loading and firing their weapons from prone positions. Commands, instead of being voice commands, were a system of bugle calls and drumbeats. Through Wallace's disciplined guidance, the Guards won a reputation as one of the finest military organizations in the state. And when the Civil War broke out, the Montgomery Guard formed the core of the 11th Indiana Volunteer Infantry Regiment.

11th Regiment Indiana Zouaves
(From non-copyrighted webpage.)

Wallace, as noted, also yearned to throw his hat into the political arena. Therefore, shortly after moving to Crawfordsville, he became an active member of the Montgomery County Democratic Party. The Democrats were the dominant party in Indiana at the time, but part of Wallace's motivation for joining them was due to his reaction against the Whig's endorsement of Zachary Taylor (against whom he still held a grudge concerning his comment about Indiana's troops).

The Democrats were strict constitutionalists who believed in limited government and were suspicious of anything that threatened their liberty. However, their love of liberty was reserved for whites only. This then made them vulnerable on the issue of slavery. With their support of the Kansas-Nebraska Act, the Democrats seemed to be developing into proponents of slavery, or at least, supporters of the status quo for the "property" rights of slaveholders. (The Kansas-Nebraska Act was passed by the U.S. Congress on May 30, 1854 and allowed people in the territories of Kansas and Nebraska to decide for themselves whether or not to allow slavery.)

While Wallace opposed slavery, he found abolitionists "fanatics and wild men; and, worse, while enemies of slavery, they were also conspirators against the Union." Furthermore, he could not blame the South alone for slavery, any more than "an unborn child is responsible for the sins of its parents." Since slavery was acknowledged and protected in the Constitution, it was a national institution. With his legal mind, he found the right of the ownership of a slave more tangible than the slave's natural right to freedom. For all his lifelong sympathies for the oppressed, Wallace was no rebel, no advocate of civil disobedience. Thus, he committed himself to "insistence upon observance of the laws as a first duty .... [and] while they endured, social good and the life of the Republic required every citizen to submit to them." (Wallace, *An Autobiography*, 1906.) Consequently, agreeing with Stephen Douglas—who introduced the Kansas-Nebraska Act—Wallace came to believe the issue of slavery could be a matter of local option in a territory.

*　　　*　　　*

At the age of twenty-nine, Wallace received the Democratic Party's nomination for state senator from Montgomery County. The Republican nominee was Dr. Labaree, who was considered the best physician in the county. Wallace visited every village in the county and, in the end, edged Labaree out by one hundred votes of the four thousand cast. Upon taking his seat, he introduced two pieces of legislature. One would have tightened Indiana's notoriously lax divorce law. The second bill called for a change in the method by which U.S. Senators were to be elected. Instead of having Senators picked by state legislatures, they would be elected by voters. While both bills went down in defeat, the direct election of United States Senators by popular vote became the law of the land when the Seventeenth Amendment was ratified on May 13, 1912.

*   *   *

On April 12, 1861, three days following the attack on Ft. Sumter, President Lincoln called seventy-five thousand state militiamen into the service of the United States; Indiana was asked to supply six regiments of about forty-five hundred men. Shortly thereafter, Governor Morton sent word to Wallace, who was addressing a jury in the Clinton County Circuit Court at the time, "Sumter has been fired on. Come immediately." Leaving the trial in the hands of his partner, he rushed back to Indianapolis to meet with Morton. Wallace, Indiana's most prominent military man, was an obvious choice to be Indiana's adjutant-general charged with raising troops, establishing a camp for the men in Indianapolis (at the state fairground which he named Camp Morton), and appointing a camp commander whose job it was to establish camp regulations for the maintenance of security and discipline. Wallace also appointed doctors to administer physicals and a quarter-master general to acquire food, clothing, housing, and camp equipment. It took only nine days for Wallace to complete his task, at which point he resigned as Indiana adjutant-general and became a colonel of his regiment of choice, the 11th Indiana's Volunteer Infantry Regiment.

*   *   *

After less than a year in uniform, Wallace wore the twin silver stars of a major-general, the highest rank then attainable. However, his rank bore the suffix "USV," for U.S. Volunteers. During this era, it was an indication he was a "political" general as opposed to a "regular army" general. Political generals were those men who met one of the following criteria—sometimes, both. First, they lacked previous experience as a commissioned officer in the pre-Civil War regular army. Many, however, were members of their local militias and took part in annual militia encampments which consisted of socializing, fancy parades, and a small amount of drill. The second group of men had a pre-war career dominated by political, not military, service. Despite having some military experience in the Mexican War and several militias, Wallace was also very-well politically connected, thus making him a political general.

The harnessing of political generals during the Civil War was part of a long tradition of amateur military commands during each of America's wars dating back to the colonial period. Besides the perceived "natural" ability of every American to master the required military skill of battle, it made sense to harness the established reputation of popular political figures. Those men with proven political leadership and organizational skills appeared just as prepared as regular army officers to handle the political aspects of military command during a civil war: how to recruit, how to treat conquered civilians, and how to maintain support for the war. Always a good judge of character, Lincoln understood the appointment of political generals would bring political support for his policies, boost recruiting from their supporters, and bind the various factions in the North together in victorious coalitions.

As much as the regulars tried to prevent the appointment of amateur commanders during the Civil War, they could not yet stop this tradition. American presidents, congressional leaders, and state governors did not see the need to rely solely on trained military experts during times of crises—even when the very fate of the Republic appeared to rest on the ability to field an effective force. This, in part, was due to their belief that the ultimate objective of the War was not to destroy the armed forces of the South, but to reestablish federal authority and political control of contested areas. As will be discussed shortly, regulars tended to view the War only as a military problem requiring a focus on the battlefield.

Perhaps more importantly, with the locus of political power still at the state and local levels at the start of the War, the state-based system of recruitment proved to be highly effective during the War when compared to the recurring efforts made at the federal level. Also, many northern state governments believed they had the right to appoint generals whenever their respective volunteer militias were federalized because their state constitutions dictated that militia and volunteer generals would be appointed by the governor or elected by the commissioned officers in their respected brigades.

Regular army generals were those men who were selected based on their military qualifications of either having graduated from West Point or serviced as career regulars with frontier or Mexican War experience. The study of generalship at West Point was started by Professor Dennis Hart Mahan during his first decade at West Point (1831 to 1841). Professor Mahan formulated and applied a philosophy of military education which was transmitted to the cadets through his nine-hour seminar on "The Science of War." He was also convinced the real purpose of West Point was to try and keep alive military science, so it did not die out during long periods of peace, thereby assuring the country would remain responsive to national emergencies. In 1847, he published *Advanced Guard, Outpost, and Detachment Service of Troops with the Essential Principles of Strategy, and Grand Tactics for the Use of Officers of the Militia and Volunteers*. Commonly known as *Outpost*, this guide shaped military thought for two generations of America's professional soldiers.

Mahan drew his grand scheme from the ideas of Baron Henri Antoine Jomini, the first great military thinker to analyze the Napoleonic way of war. Underlying all of his, and in time Mahan's, theories was a fundamental principle which he advocated in four maxims (Major Francis S. Jones, 1985):

(1) To throw by strategic movements the mass of an army successively, upon the decisive points of a theater of war, and also upon the communications of the enemy as much as possible without compromising one's own.

(2) To maneuver to engage fractions of the hostile army with the bulk of one's forces.

(3) On the battlefield, to throw the mass of the forces upon the decisive point, or upon that portion of the hostile line which it is of the first importance to overthrow.

(4) To so arrange that these masses shall not only be thrown upon the decisive point, but that they shall engage at the proper time and with energy.

As shown, Jomini's overall outlook encouraged a military contest between two armies which avoided rashness by thorough and time-consuming preparations. Consequently, when later applied during the Civil War, the approach proved to be antithetical to the political needs of a wartime government. It would also lead to frustration for the Lincoln administration and a public that waited impatiently for news of victories.

One student of Mahan who continued the development of his military theory was Henry Wager Halleck. (Early in the Civil War, Halleck commanded operations in the Western Theater from 1861 until 1862 which include the Battle of Shiloh. In July 1862, Lincoln appointed Halleck General-in-Chief of all Union forces only to demote him to Chief-of-Staff in the spring of 1864.) After graduating from West Point in 1839, and touring France in 1854, Halleck published *Elements of Military Art and Science* which expanded Mahan's call for trained general commanders to replace, once and for all, political generals. Halleck's contempt for political generals can be seen in a letter written to William T. Sherman on April 29, 1864: "It seems impossible to prevent" politically appointed amateurs from gaining significant army commands, [and] "it seems little better than murder to give important commands to men such as [Nathaniel] Banks, [Benjamin] Butler, [John] McClenard, [Franz] Sigel, and Lew Wallace."

CHAPTER 5: *Romney, Virginia*

On April 26, 1861, Governor Morton commissioned officers for Indiana's first six Civil War regiments, including Wallace as a colonel. All six regiments enlisted for a term of three months, and the 11th Indiana, at least, received its arms on that same day. Morton forwarded the appropriate paperwork to President Lincoln, who was "greatly gratified" to accept the officers and soldiers from the Hoosier state.

*　　　*　　　*

As the Civil War started, states decided to be aligned with the North or South. Kentucky was the one true exception; people chose neutrality. They felt they could not fully side with the North because Kentucky was a slave holding state with sympathies and connections to the South—both economic and personal. However, the people of the state also strongly believed in and supported the nation the Founding Fathers created.

In Indiana, Governor Morton worried raiding parties from Kentucky would cross the river into Indiana, and that boats on the Ohio would begin carrying contraband war supplies south to the Confederacy. Due to these concerns, the 11th Indiana's first order was for Wallace to take his regiment to Evansville, Indiana on the Ohio River between Louisville, Kentucky, and Cairo, Illinois. Once there, the 11th Indiana was to "establish a search of boats passing down the Ohio River." Few boat captains presented problems, so the boring assignment allowed Wallace and his officers valuable time for tactical training—four hours a day for company drill and another four hours a day for battalion drill. The new soldiers grumbled at such forced drill, but they improved in skill and endurance, which Wallace knew would ultimately be to their benefit. Also, alarms were sounded at night to train the men to instantly respond in the face of an approaching enemy.

Wallace may have succeeded in preparing his troops for battle, but he was growing tired of watching boats on the Ohio River. To remedy the situation, he pulled political strings to get his next assignment by contacting his prominent brother-in-law Senator Henry S. Lane. Lane went to Lincoln in early June on Wallace's behalf whereby Wallace and the 11th Indiana received new marching orders.

*   *   *

Wallace and his men were eager to leave Indiana and got their wish when General Winfield Scott ordered the 11th Indiana to proceed by rail to Cumberland, Maryland. Cumberland was on the Baltimore and Ohio Railroad between Grafton, Virginia and Hagerstown, Maryland. The B&O was a crucial Union transportation link connecting Baltimore and Washington D.C. with Indianapolis, Louisville, and Saint Louis. It would also become a primary means of transporting troops and supplies between the East and the West. The problem faced by the Union was that the railroad ran through north-western Virginia (now West Virginia) from Harpers Ferry to the Ohio River. As feared, on April 19, the Virginian Militia seized Harpers Ferry, and a month later was ordered to defend north-western Virginia to prevent the Union seizure of the railroad.

The Hoosier regiment left Evansville on June 5 and traveled by train to Indianapolis, then to Cincinnati, and finally to

Grafton. Upon their arrival, Wallace was briefed on the local situation by the Union Commander—between 1,300 to 2,000 Confederates were in Romney Virginia, only a day's march from Cumberland. (In fact, it was only 500 men.) When the 11th Indiana arrived in Cumberland on June 10, Wallace found orders containing permission to "capture or rout" Confederate forces in the Cumberland area. It took Wallace only a moment to decide he would mount a surprise attack on Romney.

To deceive any Confederates who may have been watching, Wallace ordered two companies off the train to make camp. The majority of his regiment, still on the train, headed back the 26 miles to New Creek (now Keyser). Their march would take them over two mountain ridges of one thousand to fifteen hundred feet, across several streams, and through Sheetz's Mill (today Headsville). For the last few miles, the road wound through the Mechanicsburg Gap and then sloped down to a covered bridge that crossed the South Branch of the Potomac River.

ROMNEY BATTLE-GROUND.[1]

Once over the bridge, the road went up Cemetery Hill and into Romney.

Wallace:

In the discussion [beforehand], we considered every objection to the movement. Forty-six miles, counting an immediate return as part of the march, would be unprecedented for infantry in one day; nevertheless, reducing the problem to one of physical endurance, we decided that the month of hard Zouave drilling just undergone at Evansville was to be treated as training sufficient for the task; besides which the men should travel light as possible.

About four o'clock in the afternoon, with eight companies, in all quite five hundred men, the march from New Creek to Romney began. Knapsacks, blankets, and haversacks were discarded, and word given out that there was no hope of breakfast or dinner except we took the town. Silence was enjoined [ordered], [and] if a gun were fired, unless by my order, he who did it should be summarily drummed out of the service. With one of the guides, I took place at the head of the column on foot, like all the rest, thinking by my example to stimulate the weary and faint of heart.

[While on the march] we came upon a straggling hamlet. In one house a light was burning, and, as luck would have it, a woman opened a door

attracted by the commotion among the dogs;
hearing us in passage, she screamed. In a
minute the population was [awake]. Then a man
led an unsaddled horse out of a back gate,
and, by paths known to himself, rode hard as
he could go to town [Romney].

Hardly had the order of march been [given
after a short delay at a mountain stream two
miles from Romney] when a party of horsemen,
probably a[forward of pickets], appeared at
the top of a low hill and fired upon my
advance-guard, who engaged them [courageously]
and drove them off unassisted. Then I knew a
surprise was no longer to be hoped.

On the side of the hill, facing us and
probably a mile away, stretched a line of men
1,000 to 1,200 carefully ordered, their arms
glittering in the sunlight. In the center two
field-pieces were conspicuous, as doubtless it
was intended they should be.

Calling a halt, I ... noticed on the farther
side a two-story red brick house ... It
appeared deserted... [yet] I regarded it
something to beware of ... The advance-guard
... was directed to rush the bridge and
observe the house from behind the embankment
on the other side. Sure enough, upon their
showing, a fire opened upon them ... Then I
led the first company across [the bridge] ...
Making use of a ditch by the roadside, my men
speedily [took possession] of the offending

premises, but, sorry to say, not the
occupants. They were too quick in getting
away.

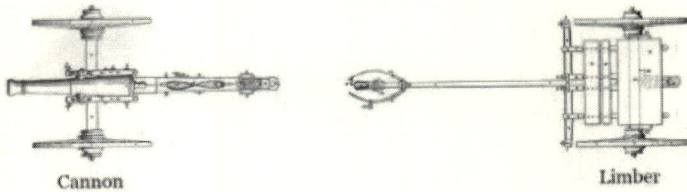

Cannon

Limber

Once the brick house was taken, Wallace ordered five companies to the double-quick up the meadow-smooth hill to the
right of the Romney road, intending to get around the line of
Confederate soldier's left flank and cut off their retreat. After a
short distance, they found a deep ravine in their path. "To my
Zouaves it was scarcely an obstruction," Wallace remarked.
Hardly had his men stepped within rifle range, the Confederates limbered up their cannon and withdrew over the hill. (A
limber is the detachable fore-part of a gun carriage, consisting
of two wheels, an axle, and a shaft to which the horses are
attached.) As Wallace's men passed over the brow of the hill,
they found the Confederates had withdrawn out of Romney,
followed by most of the white citizens. Having no cavalry,
pursuit was out of the question.

After the men of the 11th Indiana searched all the houses and
arrested about eight suspicious individuals, they requested
bread, butter, milk, and edibles from the remaining citizens.
Being as most of the remaining people were slaves, they were
eager to provide a feast for the hungry soldiers from the
pantries and smoke-houses of the vacant homes. And while
Wallace insisted that all homes, barns and other buildings be

left intact, he did confiscate three wagons with their teams and tents, equipment, uniforms, and large assortment of surgical stores left behind by the fleeing Confederates. The 11th Indiana's return march to New Creek was forced. Wallace claimed there was not a mile on the road that did not offer a half dozen positions for ambush. Soon after arriving, about 11 p.m., the men boarded the train for Cumberland.

An important impact Wallace's raid had was to force the Confederates occupying Harpers Ferry to evacuated on June 18 to Winchester. Their commanding officer, General Joseph Johnston considered Winchester to be a more defensible position. On July 5, the 11th Indiana was ordered to join General Robert Patterson of Pennsylvania, whose orders were to keep Johnston's 10,000 men at Winchester from marching east to the battle that was forming at Bull Run (Battle of First Manassas). Patterson, however, was in no position to act. Most of his troops had enlisted for only three months, and the terms of service of eighteen of his twenty-four regiments were due to expire. Also, their uniforms and shoes were worn out and they had not been paid; consequently, they were in no mood to fight. To make matters worse, he had only one battery of artillery (six cannons). While Patterson contemplated his plight, the Confederates moved out of Winchester, headed for Bull Run, and played an important part in defeating the Union forces in what became known as the "great skedaddle." (Many historians blame Patterson, due to not containing Johnston's movement, for the Union's defeat on Bull Run.)

With the Confederates gone from the Cumberland area, Wallace and his 11th Indiana returned to Indianapolis and were mustered out on August 2, 1861. Wallace then faced the task of reorganizing the 11th as a three-year regiment. He had little trouble recruiting new members for what had become a famous regiment. Although a small skirmish in the war, Wallace's "splendid dash on Romney," as President Lincoln called the battle, drew immediate applause from a public starved, after two months of a peaceful war (expected only to last 90-days), for news of fighting.

CHAPTER 6: Paducah, Kentucky

Once back in Indiana, not only did Wallace busy himself with reorganizing the 11th Indiana as a three-year regiment, he was also to present a speech for the Douglas Democrats. Preoccupied with raising his new regiment, he instead sent a letter to be read. In it he warned Democrats their efforts should be directed at ending the rebellion and avoiding those who were against the policies of the Lincoln administration. He also insisted the war was not for "negro-liberty," but "our own liberty," inseparable from our Constitution and Union.

————

Due to the possibility of civil war in Kentucky, and the southern invasion of Tennessee, in August and early September 1861, the 11th Indiana was sent to Paducah, Kentucky, where it spent the winter of 1861-62. Seizing Paducah, where the Tennessee River joins the Ohio River, would counteract any confederate movement to the region. Furthermore, Paducah strongly supported the Southern cause.

On September 7, General Charles F. Smith was placed in command of Paducah. Smith was one of the most admired officers in the antebellum army. After graduating from West Point in 1825, he remained in the army, became commandant of cadets at West Point, and served gallantly in the Mexican War. Grant, who had been a cadet under Smith, found him to be the perfect soldier. Wallace, too, was impressed with Smith upon arriving at Paducah and, at first, got on well with him.

Three days after arriving at Paducah, Wallace learned he had been promoted to brigadier-general in late July. While he claimed he was surprised, he certainly must have expected the promotion—he had political connections, he strongly advocated the Union cause, and he performed well at Romney. Also helping his cause, Lincoln needed generals for the growing Union Army, and needed the support of Northern people and politicians. One way to achieve this was to appoint "political generals." As noted by historian Gail Stephens, this promotion may have been, in some ways, a disservice to Wallace. "It is ... unfortunate that he did not serve longer at the regimental level. He would have had time to season and to learn more from his superiors, especially the estimable Smith. As it was, his quick rise probably reinforced Wallace's natural arrogance and his tendencies to work outside the system."

To Wallace's credit, he did experience doubts and anxiety with commanding a brigade after being in the army just five months. A regiment had between 400-1,000 men; a brigade had between 1,000-3,500 men, and between three to five regiments under its command. To learn what his new rank entailed, he consulted Smith. Smith gave Wallace a copy of the *U.S. Army Regulations* and a lecture making clear success was virtually guaranteed by obedience to orders. Echoing Jomini and Mahan, he told Wallace the greatest military genius possesses an aptitude for both planning and executing military operations. All the labor of an office should be directed toward preparing for battle, and a commander must then fight. In a move that would become Wallace's habit, instead of respecting Smith's decision to place the 11th Indiana in a different brigade from Wallace's, Wallace went above Smith's head and wrote the Secretary of War requesting that two regiments of the Indiana troop be placed under his command: the 11th and 23rd. In October, Wallace would again use political channels to help the 23rd get needed trousers and overcoats. He had grown frustrated when army channels kept his quartermaster from being allowed to travel to Saint Louis for supplies.

Wallace spent most of the time drilling his new brigade—drill that both he and his men needed. Wallace may have been quite competent in leading a regiment into battle, but command-ing a brigade with up to five regiments was a skill he would have to learn. He also soon discovered the 23rd Indiana was in need of a good bit of preparation before being sent into battle. Besides establishing a school of instruction for the colonel and his officers, Wallace devoted time every day drilling the regiment himself. Yet, he found the work hard and monotonous, and constantly complained about both Grant's and Smith's inaction in confronting the Confederates. Twice he sent letters to Governor Morton wondering, "For God's sake, if they have appointed me a brigadier, get me a command and let me work." When nothing transpired, he wrote Interior Secretary Caleb Smith insisting he "consented" to be sent to Paducah because he thought there would be fighting, and proposed the two Indiana regiments of his brigade be sent and placed with brigades in Washington D.C. Nothing happened, except a bit of trouble that put Smith in a bad light.

*　　*　　*

When Grant moved in to take control of Paducah, he informed the citizens, in keeping with Lincoln's policies, the rights of all citizens, including slave owners and those who sympathized with the Confederacy, would be respected. Wallace, ironically, did not agree with Lincoln's policy. He felt individuals who declared their adherence to the Confederacy cause were undeserving of protection. This explains his decision to take over

an empty house owned by R. Woolfolk, a southern sympa-
thizer, to house the sick men of his cavalry. Not only did
Woolfolk complain to Smith, but someone in his family put a
Confederate flag out which led to the following firestorm. At
least three versions of this story exist, * but what follows is one
that appears in the November 25, 1861 *St. Louis Democrat*:

Trouble at Paducah

On Tuesday last, a Secessionist in Paducah, by
the name of Woolfolk, hung a secession flag
out of his window as some of our troops were
passing by, and hurrahed for Jeff Davis. The
man had done the same thing before on several
occasions, and the matter was reported to
Brig.-Gen. C.F. Smith, but he refused to
interfere. This refusal of Gen. Smith caused
great indignation among the troops, and doubts
of his loyalty were freely expressed in
Paducah.

The matter having been reported to Gen.
Wallace, he sent his Aid-de-Camp with a squad
of men, to order the traitorous flag to be
taken in, and, if Woolfolk refused, then to
take it in, and erect the Stars and Stripes
over his house. Woolfolk, knowing that Gen.
Smith was senior officer, refused to obey Gen.
Wallace's order, whereupon Wallace's aids
forcibly took down the rebel flag, and hoisted
the Stars and Stripes in its stead.
In the meantime, Woolfolk having appealed to
Gen. Smith, the latter sent his aid, Lieut.
Price, to order Gen. Wallace to have the Stars

and Stripes taken down from Woolfolk's house.
Wallace refused to obey the order and sent
word to Smith that the flag should not be
taken down while there was a live man in his
brigade. Wallace's aid said that Woolfolk
should sleep under a loyal flag one night,
anyhow. Smith's aid replied that he did not
consider that any great honor. Whereupon
Wallace's aid knocked down Smith's aid. Gen.
Paine sent Wallace assurances of his
cooperation.

As Gen. Smith had nobody but his discomfited
Lieutenant to enforce his order "the old flag
still waves."

The next day Gen. Smith issued a general order
complaining of this breach of military
discipline, remonstrating against like
occurrences in the future, and reminding the
troops that they were sent into Kentucky as
protectors of a loyal State, and that
moderation and forbearance should be exercised
toward unarmed enemies, and that they should
ever show themselves the champions of law and
order.

Another account says that Gen. Wallace went
with his whole regiment to tear down the
obnoxious flag, and that he made a
congratulatory speech to his soldiers after
the affair was over. Also, that a Missouri
regiment started with a fire-engine to wash
out Gen. Smith's headquarters, which they were

dissuaded from doing by Gen. Wallace. There
was much feeling against Gen. Smith."

What is interesting about this event is that it fell on the heels
of a move to have Smith removed from command by another
of Smith's volunteer subordinates, General Eleazer Paine.
Paine was an Illinois lawyer who held influence over many
mid-western newspapers. Like Wallace, the clash was over
Smith's West Pointers' belief that time was needed to prepare
for any campaign, and the volunteers' belief—generally shared
by the public—that time was being wasted. While there is no
evidence Wallace was involved in this, his brother-in-law,
Senator Lane, did try to have Smith removed.

* See *Paducah and the Civil War* by John Philip Cashon

———

Volunteer troops and volunteer officers, many of them men of
political influence, would be taken at their word if they wrote
to home-town newspapers or to congressmen. This became
another point of contention between political and regular
generals. No regular officer, even in some cases political officers, could consider himself safe. It must be remembered,
about one-third of the United States Army officers resigned
their federal commissions to join the Confederacy. Who could
be sure which regular Northern general might in fact hold
Southern sympathies. Consequently, the war was being fought
in an era of unlimited suspicion—simply to be suspected was
just about as bad as to be convicted.

In relation to General Paine, an Indianapolis man signing
himself simply "A Friend of Justice" wrote to Smith on
December 2 saying men in the 11th Indiana were sending home
word that Smith was disloyal and adding that these reports

undoubtedly originated with one of Smith's subordinates, the brand-new Brigadier-General from Indiana, Lew Wallace (Catton, 1960/2000). In a letter to a friend, Smith knew not to blame Wallace, writing "a poor devil as a man or as a soldier by the name of Paine hatched a base conspiracy to oust me from command on the ground of ... disloyalty, etc., etc." Catton also pointed out, in a civil war, unquestioned loyalty to the government's cause was the one virtue that counted more than all others combined, and it was precisely the professional soldier, temperamentally unable to imagine his loyalty could possibly come under suspicion, who was the most likely to get into trouble. Trouble of this sort plagued Charles P. Stone, Fitz-John Porter, George McClellan, Don Carlos Buell and others.

———

One other event at Paducah, in which Wallace was actually an innocent party, caused problems for Grant. In the end of October, Grant visited Paducah to confer with Smith. During that time, he stayed in Wallace's house. One night during this stay, he, Smith, and Wallace passed an evening together where there were cigars, some liquor, stories and singing until the late hours, but no intoxication on the part of any of the three men. Regardless, one of Wallace's regimental chaplains was privy to the event, leaked and exaggerated accounts of the evening, claiming "an orgy, a beastly drunken revel led by both Grant and Smith." Unknown to Wallace was Grant's reputation for drinking established during his first term of military service. While Wallace had no part in the stories of the night which appeared in numerous papers, Grant's staff placed the blame on Wallace. This dislike for Wallace by Grant's staff would be detrimental to his career after the Battle of Shiloh.

* * *

In December 1861, Susan Wallace paid a brief visit to her husband at Paducah and was horrified at her first exposure to slavery. When a scouting party rescued a runaway from being torn apart by bloodhounds, Susan wrote to a friend that "the brutal man everyone despises is a hunter of slaves; no one notices the slave jails, the whipping posts are out of sight, so are the low whites who do the flogging, but they are here, in Kentucky, the mildest State holding the 'patriarchal institution'." Describing the horrors of slavery, she emphatically rejected the often-repeated claim "that slaves love slavery." After Susan returned home, Lew rejected his former anti-abolitionist stand and confessed in a letter to her that "However we may go into the war, we shall come out of it abolitionists" (see Morsberger, 1980).

CHAPTER 7: Fort Henry & Fort Donelson

Union forces in late 1861 were organized into two separate commands: General Don Carlos Buell commanding 45,000 men from a headquarters at Louisville, Kentucky, and General Halleck commanding 91,000 men from his headquarters at St. Louis, Missouri. The Confederate forces facing Buell and Halleck were 43,000 ill-equipped troops under General Albert Sidney Johnston. Charged with defending a line that stretched for more than 500 miles from western Virginia to the border of Kansas, Johnston's forces mostly lay east of the Mississippi River. They occupied a system of forts and camps from Cumberland Gap in western Virginia through Bowling Green, Kentucky, to Columbus, Kentucky, on the Mississippi. Rivers and railroads provided Johnston with most of his interior lines of communications, since most of the roads were virtually impassable in winter. To protect a lateral railroad where it crossed two rivers in Tennessee, the Confederates built two earthen forts, Fort Henry on the Tennessee River and Fort Donelson on the Cumberland River just south of the boundary between Kentucky and Tennessee.

At the beginning of 1862, Halleck and Buell were supposed to be cooperating but had yet to do so effectively. Meanwhile, in Halleck's department, General Ulysses S. Grant proposed a river expedition up the Tennessee to take Fort Henry. After some hesitancy, Halleck approved a plan for a joint Army-Navy expedition. On January 30, 1862, he directed 15,000 men under Grant, supported by armored gunboats and river craft of the U.S. Navy under a flag officer, Andrew H. Foote, to "take and hold Fort Henry." Fort Henry had been built the previous summer at an ill-advised location. On the eastern bank of the Tennessee River, it lay on such low bottom land it became a submerged swamp in high water. Realizing the vulnerability of the fort, the Confederates began the construction of another fort, Fort Heiman, on the higher ground on the western side of the river.

———

Grant landed his troops below Fort Henry and, together with Foote's seven gunboats, moved against the Confederate position on February 6. Responding to the Union's naval bombardment, General Lloyd Tilghman yielded Fort Henry and sent most of his men to Fort Donelson. Muddy roads delayed the Union Army's advance, but Foote's seven gunboats plunged ahead and in a short firefight caused the remaining defenders of Fort Henry to surrender. The Tennessee River now lay open to Foote's gunboats all the way to northern Alabama.

———

At the time of the bombardment, Wallace was under the command General Charles F. Smith. Grant had sent Smith to move his division along the opposite of the Tennessee River overlooking Fort Henry. (The purpose was to join in the gunboats' bombardment.)

Wallace:

Suddenly — somewhere between twelve and one o'clock — we were startled by the report of a heavy gun up the river. I could see nothing of the river up or down; yet I knew that the leading boat, the flag-ship probably, had turned the corner of Panther Island [which

screened the approach to Fort Henry], and
found itself in instant engagement with the
fort. I could fancy them, then, the four in
armor, one by one rounding the island, giving
space to the left as they made the turn, in
line directly, and moving forward, bow on,
firing — firing, for that matter, while the
maneuver was in progress.

In a short time the ships passed us. I could
tell that by the firing. Then they increased
their speed. Presently they were between us
and the fort — that we knew because the shells
of the latter, over-elevated, sailed roaring
and screaming into the tree-tops, darkening
the air with fragments of limbs. Indeed, the
margin separating us from the line of hostile
fire was at times preciously narrow, but the
effect was to energize everybody in the march.

Much I doubt if there ever was a march
distinguished like that one; for what with the
cannonading of the fleet and that of the fort,
the interchange became an almost uninter-
mittent thunder which the ponderous missiles
in flight converted into an [attribute of
hell*] indescribably awful. And to make the
situation more peculiar, we could see nothing
of the fight on the river — to us hastening
through the woods, it was all smoke, sound,
and fury … Once we stopped to improvise a
bridge by which to pass our guns. At last we
were approaching Heiman … General Smith, [who
was riding with me] said, "Halt. The firing

has stopped." I suggested pushing on with a
regiment. He[emphatically*] refused. On a
little farther a horseman from the front rode
to him and reported Heiman evacuated.

[Upon entering one of the tents, I found]
Dinner was ready. I looked into a kettle yet
boiling and discovered a block of fresh pork
"done to a turn." By the kettle a pot simmer-
ed, spraying the air with the aroma of coffee.
A pone of corn-bread freshly baked adorned a
bench nearby, and under the lid of a mess-box
rudely constructed a little rummaging
disclosed salt, pepper, vinegar, and white
sugar in lump.

As with Mexico and Romney, Wallace was curious how
"downright hard fighting was always" just beyond his grasp.

*Here Wallace used the word, "infernalsim." Perhaps the root word being
'infernal," but his use appears to be self-created.
**The word "emphatically," replaces the word "peremptorily."

———

After the capture of Fort Henry, Grant telegraphed Halleck: "I
shall take and destroy Fort Donelson on the 8th." However,
inclement weather, the need of supplies, and the repair of
Foote's gunboats, delayed the Union movement until February
12. This delay gave Johnston time to send for reinforcements
under the command of Brigadier-General Gideon Pillow to
Donelson with orders to hold the fort only long enough to
allow the remaining Confederate forces in Kentucky to fall
back into Tennessee and reestablish their defensive line. Upon

his arrival, Pillow realized that if Donelson fell, the next stop for Union gunboats would be Nashville, Tennessee. After a brief survey of the fort, Pillow sent a message to Johnston that read, "I will never surrender the position." Johnston, seeing the likelihood in Pillow's prediction, sent Brigadier-Generals John B. Floyd and Simon Bolivar Buckner with additional troops to defend the fort.

———

On February 10, Grant held a Council of War to determine whether the army should move immediately on the fort or wait for reinforcements. While it was decided to move immediately, Wallace had his doubts. In writing to his wife, Susan, the next day, he stated, "It is wonderful how little we know in advance of the conditions of the enemy." If Wallace saw a lack of judgment on the part of the other generals, he was deeply angered when he was informed he would be left behind to command Fort Henry. While the friendship between Wallace and Smith was growing thin, Smith trusted Wallace to hold the rear in case of attack from Confederate Polk and his 20,000 men still in the vicinity. Again, to his wife Wallace wrote, "Through old Smith, I am left behind ... I have been sick from rage since yesterday ... My patience with old Smith is now 'played out' ... I have been too modest and patient." Unable to control his anger, Wallace sent Grant a note of protest. Grant, who responded quickly, assured Wallace that as soon his troops were called up, he would be given a division of his own. At midnight on February 13, Wallace received orders to immediately form up and march to Donelson. While happy to be called up, he was informed he would indeed gain a division, but it would not include his 11th Indiana.

*   *   *

At the start of the attack, Grant was certain his land force, combined with the gunboats, would take Donelson, but as Grant would soon discover, the fort was a strong position. The main earthwork stood 100 feet above the river, and its outlying system of rifle pits covered an area of 100 acres. The fort also consisted of two water batteries which faced directly down the Cumberland River. These batteries consisted of twelve guns including one powerful ten-inch Columbiad which fired a 238-pound shell.

10-inch Columbiad at Ft. Donelson

Grant and Foote first attempted to reduce the fort by naval bombardment on February 14. Although Foote's gunboats pressed to within four hundred yards of the batteries, the powerful and well-sighted Confederate guns inflicted immense damage on the Union flotilla, sending it back down river. It would now be up to Grant's army, many of whom had never seen battle before, to take the fort.

Upon his arrival at Grant's headquarters, Wallace was put in charge of the 3rd Division which numbered approximately six thousand men. He was also told he was to take the position in the center of the line for the upcoming battle. General John McClernand's division was placed on the right of the line, and General Smith's division was on the left.

Quite unexpectedly, on Saturday morning, February 15, about 5:45 a.m., there was heavy firing immediately to the Union front. The Confederates had decided to cut their way through the Union lines on the Wynne's Ferry and Forge roads, with the intent of moving the army at Nashville. Union pickets were driven back, and in less than twenty minutes the right of McClernand's command was actively engaged. "It was one of those fierce onslaughts which the Rebels made so often during the war, gallant, desperate, but unavailing; it lasted from a quarter of six in the morning until nearly eleven o'clock" (Brevet-Major Henry C. Hicks, 1896).

By 8 a.m., the right of General McClernand's line had been driven in toward its center, fully three-quarters of a mile. McClernand sent a message to Wallace, who was commanding the center, for support. Wallace responded by saying he had orders from Grant to hold his own positions at all hazards; he therefore declined to forward reinforcements. He did, though, send a messenger to Grant's headquarters only to learn Grant had gone to consult Foote on the gunboats. (In his memoirs, Grant wrote, "I had no idea that there would be any engagement on land unless I brought it myself." He was wrong, as McClernand's division learned.) Upon receiving no reinforcements, General McClernand sent Wallace a second message stating the enemy had turned his flanks—pushing him away from Forge Road and parallel along Wynne's Ferry Road—thus endangering his whole command. Without orders,

Wallace 1) sent "Colonel Thayer's 3rd Brigade up the road to where the ridge dips towards the rebel works, and directed the colonel to form a new line of battle at a right angle with the old one, 2) sent in Company A, Chicago Light Artillery, and 3) dispatched a messenger to inform General Smith of the state of affairs and asked him for assistance" (Wallace, February 12-16, 1862).

Wallace, February 12-16, 1862:

The head of Colonel Thayer's column filed right double-quick. Lieutenant Wood, commanding the artillery company sent for, galloped up with a portion of his battery and posted his pieces … A line of reserve was also formed at a convenient distance in rear of the first line … Scarcely had this formation been made when the enemy attacked, coming up the road and through the shrubs and trees … [Our men] met the storm, no man flinching, and their fire was terrible. To say they did well is not enough. Their conduct was splendid. They alone repelled the charge. Colonel Cruft, as was afterwards ascertained, from his position saw the enemy retire to their works pell-mell and in confusion.

About 3 o'clock General Grant rode up the hill and ordered an advance and attack on the enemy's left, while General Smith attacked their right. At General McClernand's request I [undertook] the proposed assault. (McClernand's men were exhausted and lacked ammunition to keep fighting.)

Examining the ground forming the position to be assailed (Wallace saw that in order to retake the Wynn's Ferry and Forge roads, his men would have to drive the Confederates off the ridge they still occupied in front of the roads and back into their works), I quickly arranged my column of attack … Well aware of the desperate character of the enterprise, I informed the regiments of it as they moved on, and they answered with cheers and cries of "Forward!" "Forward!" and I gave the word … My directions as to the mode of attack were general, merely to form columns of regiments, march up the hill which was the point of assault, and deploy as occasion should require.

While the fighting was in progress an order reached me through Colonel Webster to retire my column, as a new plan of operations was in contemplation for the next day. If carried out, the order would have compelled me to give up the hill so hardly recaptured. Satisfied that the [Grant] did not know of our success when he issued the direction, I assumed the responsibility of disobeying it, and held the battle ground that night … [The] next morning about daybreak Lieutenant Ware, my aide-de-camp, conducted Colonel Thayer's brigade to the foot of the hill. Lieutenant Wood's battery was also ordered to the same point, my intention being to storm the intrenchments about breakfast time. While making disposition for that purpose a white flag made its appearance. The result was that I … informed

General Grant that the place was surrendered
and my troops in possession of the town and
all the works on the right.

Soon thereafter, Grant received a note from the Confederate
commander, General Simon Bolivar Buckner, a fellow West
Point graduate. Buckner asked for a meeting to discuss terms
to end the fighting. Soon afterward Grant sent his famous
message: "No terms except unconditional and immediate
surrender can be accepted. I propose to move immediately
upon your works." A legend and a nickname "Unconditional
Surrender Grant" were born.

The victory of Fort Donelson was of enormous importance.
The Confederacy lost an army and its entire western line of
defense. Seven days later, on February 23, the Union forces
captured Nashville. The taking of Forts Henry and Donelson
was the first major Union victory and provided a much-needed
boost of morale after the misery of Manassas. It led the people
of the North to believe the war would end soon; the *New York
Herald* predicted the rebellion would end within twenty days.
Wallace was under the same impression, writing his wife the
day after the city's fall, "Verily, the war looks over to me. When
we break the centre of the rebellion, as we have done, we break
the monster's heart. Don't be surprised if we all come home to
sit down under our 'vine and fig tree' to eat, be merry, smoke
and talk out battles over again, with nobody to shake a fist at
but England." The victory of Donelson opened the way to
Shiloh.

*   *   *

In their official reports of the battle, Grant gave most of the
credit for the victory to Smith, his old West Point teacher. Of
Wallace, Grant wrote, he "contributed to hold the enemy

within his lines." Smith said nothing of Wallace's efforts, and peculiarly, McClernand implied Wallace had been unaccountably absent from the field at his crucial moment of need. Despite these omissions, Wallace received his share of the glory. The citizens of Crawfordsville sent him a beautiful sword in honor of his victory. Many Northern newspapers ran stories about the dashing young general from Indiana. To counter what he felt was the "infamous robberies" of credit in other newspapers, he sent a copy of his official report to Benson John Lossing who was writing and illustrating his *The Pictorial History of the Civil War in The United States of America, Volume 2*. And in March, at his brother-in-law Senator Lane's prompting, he was promoted to major-general, the highest rank then possible. Only Halleck and Grant, who received the rank before Wallace, out-ranked him.

CHAPTER 8: The Battle of Shiloh

PART ONE

By mid-February 1862, United States forces had won decisive victories in the West at Mill Springs, Kentucky, and Forts Henry and Donelson in Tennessee. These successes opened the way for invasion up the Tennessee River to sever Confederate rail communications along the important Memphis & Charleston and Mobile & Ohio railroads. Forced to abandon Kentucky and Middle Tennessee, General Johnston, moved to protect his rail communications by concentrating his scattered forces around the small town of Corinth in northeast Mississippi, strategic crossroads of the Memphis & Charleston and the Mobile & Ohio.

Shiloh Church
Frank Leslie Famous Leaders and Battle Scenes of the Civil War
Florida Center for Instructional Technology
Used with permission.

In March, General Halleck ordered armies under Generals Ulysses S. Grant and Don Carlos Buell southward to cut the railroad lines. Grant traveled up the Tennessee River by steamboat, disembarking his Army of the Tennessee at Pittsburg Landing, 22 miles northeast of Corinth. There he established a base of operations on a plateau (Shiloh Hill) west of the river, with his forward camps under the command of William Tecumseh Sherman, posted two miles inland around a log church called Shiloh Meeting House. Halleck had specifically instructed Grant not to engage the Confederates until he had been reinforced by Buell's Army of the Ohio, then marching overland from Nashville. Once combined, the two armies would advance on Corinth and permanently break western Confederate railroad communications.

General Johnston, aware of Federal intentions of attacking Corinth, planned to smash Grant's army at Pittsburg Landing before Buell arrived. He placed his troops in motion on April 3, but heavy rain and difficulties encountered by marching large columns of troops, artillery, and heavy wagons over muddy roads delayed the attack. By nightfall, April 5, his Army of the Mississippi, nearly 44,000 men, was finally prepared for battle four miles southwest of Pittsburg Landing.

At daybreak, Sunday April 6, the Confederates stormed out of the woods and struck the forward Union camps around Shiloh Church. Grant and his nearly 40,000 men present for duty were surprised by the onslaught. The Federals soon rallied and bitter fighting consumed Shiloh Hill. Throughout the morning, Confederate brigades slowly gained ground, forcing Grant's troops to give way, grudgingly, making successive defensive stands at Shiloh Church, the Peach Orchard, Water Oaks

Pond, and within an impenetrable oak thicket to become known as the Hornet's Nest.

Despite having achieved surprise, Johnston's troops soon lost coordination as corps, divisions, and brigades became entangled. Then, at mid-afternoon, as he supervised an assault on the Union left, Johnston was struck in the right leg by a bullet and bled to death, leaving General P.G.T. Beauregard in command of the Confederate army. Grant's battered divisions retired to a strong position extending west from Pittsburg Landing where massed artillery and rugged ravines protected their front and flanks. Fighting ended at nightfall.

In his *Personal Memoirs*, Grant wrote, "General Lew Wallace, with 5,000 effective men, arrived after firing had ceased for the day, and was placed on the right. Thus night came, Wallace came, and the advance of Nelson's division came [of Buell's Army of the Ohio]; but none—until night—in time to be of material service to the gallant men who saved Shiloh on that first day against large odds. Buell's loss on the 6th of April was two men killed and one wounded, all members of the 36th Indiana infantry. The Army of the Tennessee lost on that day at least 7,000 men." Beauregard, unaware Buell had arrived, planned to finish the destruction of Grant the next day. At dawn, April 7, however, it was Grant who attacked.

Throughout the day, the combined Union armies, numbering more than 54,500 men, hammered Beauregard's depleted ranks of barely 34,000 troops. Despite mounting desperate counterattacks, the exhausted Confederates could not stem the increasingly stronger Federal tide. Forced back to Shiloh Church, Beauregard skillfully withdrew his outnumbered army to Corinth. The battered Federal forces did not press the pursuit. The Battle of Shiloh, or Pittsburg Landing, was over.

It had cost both sides a combined total of 23,746 men killed, wounded, or missing, more casualties than America had suffered in all her previous wars. The ultimate control of the railroad junction at Corinth remained in doubt.

THE BATTLE OF SHILOH, PART TWO

After the battle, as a way to protect Grant's reputation, many of Grant's staff voiced the belief Wallace disobeyed Grant's order to move to the front and somehow got lost. To this day, many historians and textbooks still claim he somehow got lost. However, upon a closer examination, it is clear the forces that prevented Wallace from arriving on the field in a timelier matter were a combination of confusing orders and Confederates pushing the Union Army away from the road Wallace had cleared.

Crump's Landing where Gen. Lew Wallace's division was stationed just prior to the Battle of Shiloh. Image courtesy of the Marian Morrison Local History Collection, Crawfordsville District Public Library.

On March 12, Wallace was ordered to Crump's Landing on the Tennessee River, approximately five miles north, or downstream from what became the main base for Grant's army, Pittsburg Landing. From there, Wallace was to observe any enemy movement in the area and continue to Bethel Station. Once at Bethel, he was to cut the Memphis & Ohio Railroad Line. This would prevent the Confederates from rushing men to Crump's Landing. By taking Crump's Landing, the Confederates could commandeer a storehouse of Union supplies and cut river communications between Savannah and Pittsburg Landing—thereby isolating Grant's headquarters from his army. Furthermore, Wallace was also to make sure Confederate General Benjamin Cheatham's forces were ousted from the area. While this task was accomplished, it was done so only after Cheatham destroyed Wallace's bridge. In addition to the troops stationed at Crump's landing, Wallace held the towns of Adamsville and Stoney Lonesome.

————

While at Crump's Landing, Wallace needed to secure a link with the rest of the army. The condition of River Road between Crump's and Pittsburg Landings was a problem. Being so close to the flooded Tennessee, much of the terrain the road crossed had turned to swampland. It would have been difficult for the transport of infantry and artillery. Also, the Confederates had dismantled the bridges along the route.

On March 22, Wallace sent out a scouting party to find all fords and by-roads suitable for transporting troops, heavy guns, and baggage wagons. While not readily usable, one was found, the Shunpike, which branched off the Crump's Landing-Purdy Road (at Stoney Lonesome) and ran southwest to Hamburg-Purdy Road, the road that crossed Owl Creek near Sherman's camp. It was determined that with a few hours work, the Overshot Mill dam could be made into a bridge over the largest watercourse, Snake Creek. Once across, the land was firm and fit for moving an army. Therefore, if Sherman needed reinforcements, or needed to retreat, the road cleared by Wallace would meet those needs. As Bruce Catton notes in his *Grant Moves South*, "[Grant] warned both Sherman and W.H.L. Wallace [no relation to Lew Wallace] that an attack at Crump's Landing seemed quite likely and that both men should be prepared to reinforce that spot at a moment's notice."

Wallace, as did Grant, believed that after the defeat at Fort Donelson, the fight had gone out of the Confederates—allowing the Union to assume the role of aggressor. This can be seen in the fact Grant did not order the construction of entrenchments, despite Halleck's orders, and failed to send out scouting parties to investigate the numerous reports of enemy sightings. As noted above, it was the Confederates who moved first and drove the Union forces back towards Pittsburg Landing. Thus, as the first day of battle wore on, Wallace's work was rendered useless, and he indeed appeared to be lost.

———

At Crump's Landing, Wallace was awakened near dawn April 6, by an orderly who informed him he heard sounds of guns up river. Wallace quickly summoned his staff officers, and from the sounds of cannon and musketry, agreed a battle was in progress. At 6:00 a.m., Wallace instructed his aide, Captain Ross, to order the brigade commands to concentrate their forces at Stoney Lonesome where they should form in readiness to march. From Stoney Lonesome, Wallace could march his division either by the partially submerged River Road to

Pittsburg Landing or by the Shunpike towards Sherman's right.

So ordered, Wallace boarded a steamboat, and when Grant's *Tigress*, arriving from Savannah, pulled alongside around 8:00 a.m., the two commanders discussed how Wallace should deploy. Wallace and his officers were sure Grant would order the 3rd Division into action, but instead Grant told Wallace, "Well, hold yourself in readiness to march upon orders received."

To which Wallace responded, "But, General, I ordered a concentration about 6:00. The division must be at Stoney Lonesome. I am ready now."

Hesitating a moment, Grant restated his orders, "Very well. Hold the division ready to march in any direction."

In Wallace's mind, "Any direction" implied either the River Road or the Shunpike.

Once Grant's gunboat had departed, Wallace and his men moved on to Stoney Lonesome, but he did leave a fresh horse for a messenger coming from the field of battle or by boat with an order to move.

Around 11:30 p.m., Captain Ross and Grant's chief quarter-master, A.S. Baxter, approached Wallace at a gallop. According to Wallace, Baxter handed him a stained piece of paper which contained the orders: "You will leave a sufficient force at Crump's Landing to guard the [supplies]; with the rest of the division march and form junction with the right of the army. Form line of battle at right angle with the river and be governed by circumstance."

After reading the message twice, Wallace asked Baxter, "Whose order is this?" Baxter said it was Grant's.

"Why is it not signed by someone?" Wallace asked.

Baxter replied, "General Grant gave me that order on the field verbally. Fearing to make a mistake in the delivery, I put the order in writing, as you see it, coming down the river. For that purpose I picked the paper from the floor in the ladies' cabin; and, not having ink, I used a pencil."

Then, once accepting the order, Wallace asked, "Now, how is the battle going?"

"We are repulsing the enemy," Baxter stated.

(During the exchange, Wallace notes that "Colonel Thayer, standing by my side, held out his hand for the paper, and I gave it to him; passing generally around then, it finally reached Adjutant-General Kneffler, who carelessly thrust it under his sword-belt and forgot and lost it." Once lost, the written order would be useless in defending Wallace's actions that day.)

Upon learning the enemy was being repulsed, Wallace assumed the right of the Union army was where the Confederates had been driven back. To reach that position on the battle field by the River Road would require a march of eight and three-quarters miles (six to Pittsburg Landing and the remainder to Sherman's division). However, the alternate route—the Shunpike—went directly toward Sherman, saving two and three-quarters miles.

Wallace:

And at noon exactly the march began, the cavalry leading … The going was swift and without incident. Past the old overshot mill, past Snake Creek, past Clear Creek, and no enemy — not a shot. Once I allowed a rest of three minutes, but before the time was up the men arose of themselves and fell in, shouting: "Forward! Forward!" For now we were nearing the fight, and with every step it made itself more distinctly present.

The last file of the rear-guard had put Clear Creek behind it, and the guard itself was stepping long and fast. [The time was] One o'clock and thirty minutes by the watch. We were doing splendidly. Then I was overtaken by a young man with a lieutenant's shoulder-straps. I noticed his horse breathing quick and splattered with mud from nostrils to fetlocks … Riding to my side, he saluted and said, "General Wallace?"

"Yes," I replied, "General Grant sends his compliments. He would like you to hurry up."

Without stopping, without a question, I returned, "My compliments to General Grant, and tell him I am making good time and will be up shortly."

The courier left me, going by the rear.
At this point, things do not seem to be adding up to Wallace.

This message was of an import to have drawn attention and led to inquiry but for the fatal answer of Captain Baxter — "We are repulsing the enemy." If the enemy is being repulsed, I had asked myself, what need is there for me … It must be for a flanking operation or pursuit. The firing had moved opaquely to our left, and I settled discussion of the circumstance, thinking of Baxter, and arguing, "The enemy has been driven from the right to which we are going, but he is still making it warm [fight hard] over on the left nearer the river."

A few minutes after two o'clock — another interruption came along. Captain Rowley, of General Grant's staff, rode up from the rear. He was greatly excited.

"I've had a devil of a time in finding you," he began.

I checked my horse. "What's the matter?"

"I've been sent to hurry you up."

"That's the second message of the kind. I don't understand it."

"Where are you going, anyhow?"

"To join Sherman."

"Sherman!"

"Yes."

He plucked my sleeve. "Come with me aside here." At the edge of the road, out of hearing, the captain broke out: "Great God! Don't you know Sherman has been driven back? Why, the whole army is within half a mile of the river, and it's a question if we are not all going to be driven into it."

Now, I would be very disingenuous not to admit myself more than shocked by this intelligence … [and] in common phrase, "Oh, he's rattled!" And I know the word is slang; nevertheless, I dare to use it because it so nearly describes the condition into which I was flung mentally … Fortunately for me, the eclipse of my faculties did not last long, and I was able presently to comprehend that, with my division, *I was actually in rear of the whole Confederate army!*

Turning to Captain Rowley, I asked him, [without appeal]: "Does General Grant send me orders?"

"Yes," said the captain, "he wants you at Pittsburg Landing — and he wants you there like hell."

How should Wallace proceed? So far as he or Rowley knew, there was no crossroad from the Shunpike to River Road. To locate one, Wallace sent two orderlies to find and commandeer any local resident who knew of a path or trail that connected the two roads. Discovering one, Wallace ordered a highly questionable time-consuming maneuver: instead of simply having his men do an about-face and begin marching, he ordered his lead regiment—now at the end of the line—to move to the front. He would later explain he wanted his best men to engage in battle first. Despite this delay, the men of the 3rd Division moved in quick-time through ravines and swamps, at times floundering and wallowing in mud and water up to their hips. It was not enough.

CHAPTER 9: The Battle of Shiloh

PART THREE

Lew Wallace's 3rd Division arrived on the battlefield around 6:30 p.m., too late to help because fighting rarely took place at night during the Civil War. The Union army had been pushed back two miles by the Confederates. General Beauregard, who had taken over for Johnson upon his death, sent a message to Confederate President Jefferson Davis that the Rebel forces had gained "a complete victory, driving the enemy from every position ... and [w]ould finish him up in the morning."

However, unknown to General Beauregard, Grant would be strengthened by the arrival of both Wallace's division and Buell's army. The next morning, April 7, Beauregard was able to muster no more than twenty thousand infantry, and every man had not only fought hard the day before, but slept poorly due to heavy rain and to the Union's constant shelling. Grant would begin the day with twenty-eight thousand fresh soldiers with a total force of about forty thousand men.

———

Toward morning an officer of the pickets brought Wallace a man able to tell him the Confederates held the crest of the opposite slope of Tighlman's Creek. With that information, about 5:30 a.m., Wallace ordered his batteries to open fire on the enemy. Wallace intended to take out the Confederate battery before ordering his troops to advance. These two were the 9th Indiana Battery, commanded by Lieutenant George

Brown located in Perry Field, and General Buell's battery
commanded by Lieutenant Charles Thurber at the north in
Russian Tenant Field. The point of attack was the Alabama
Battery, commanded by Captain William H. Ketchum. This
artillery duel lasted until about 6:30 a.m. when Ketchum
retreated.

As the artillery duel raged hot, General Grant arrived to give
the day's orders.

Wallace (from his *An Autobiography* and *Appleton's
Booklovers Magazine,* vol. vii. January-June, *1906, p. 72.)*

Presently General Grant came towards me, with
one orderly at his back. I rode to meet him.

"Good-morning," he said.

I saluted and returned his greeting.

"Are you ready to advance?"

"Ready, sir."

He glanced down the line to get its general
direction, turned his horse to the front,
waved his hand, and said:

"Well, move out that way" (directly to his
front across Tilghman Branch).

"I shall be on the extreme right then?"

"Yes."

"You are ready?"

"Yes, sir — ready."
Beyond that there was no exchange of words —
no gossip, no allusion to the affair of
yesterday's [late arrival].

General Grant then road away. When he had gone
some yards, I galloped after him.

"Pardon me, General," I said, "but is there
any special formation you would like me to
take in attacking?"

He replied, "No, I leave that to your
discretion."

"I will be supported, of course?"

"I will see to that," he said.

I would like in passing to observe, though not
in the way of complaint or accusation, that
this conversation turned out, before the day
was over, to be chiefly remarkable for what
General Grant did not tell me. Thus, he did
not tell me of the ground over which I had to
go with my division. It may be he knew nothing
of it. He did not tell me by whom I was to be
supported. He gave me no hint of the condition
of the divisions engaged the day before, or of
the order of battle now …

Above all, he did not tell me the Army of the Ohio was on the field, commander and all. Why he withheld that, when there was every reason for communicating it to me, I have never had explained.

My principal concern … had reference to the support I was to have in moving out as directed by him. His assurance that he would see to it was sufficient, and I set about the duty before me cheerfully, but with a resolution to be cautious and circumspect.

Wallace ordered his 3rd Division forward "by *echelon* of regiments," with his line at right angle to the Tennessee River.

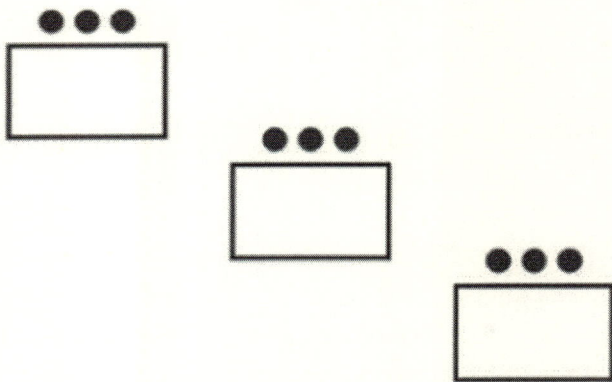

An echelon formation is a formation in which its units are arranged diagonally. Each unit is stationed behind and to the right (a "right echelon"), or behind and to the left ("left echelon"), of the unit ahead.

Advancing at approximately 6:30 a.m., against the Confederate left, Wallace's regiments moved down into a gorge 50-60 foot in depth with Tilghman's Creek at its bottom.

Wallace:

The hollow in our front was really a deep gorge having in its bottom Tilghman's Creek fringed with brush and swampy.

I gave the word forward.

The outgoing of the skirmishers (skirmishers are light infantry or cavalry soldiers stationed to act as a vanguard, flank guard, or rearguard, screening a tactical position or a larger body of friendly troops from enemy advances) reminded me of a flushing in the woods of a flock of pheasants — it was so instantaneous, so whirring-like. In my theory they were the antennae of feelers of the division in motion; and hardly had they disappeared down the hill, plunging into the gorge, when Smith's left regiment, the 11th Indiana, started forward, followed precisely as in drill by all the other regiments, one by one. In the north field, behind Thayer's brigade, I watched the movement. It was an exciting and beautiful performance all through from flank to flank, arms at right-shoulder shift, no man hanging back, and the colors imparting warmth and splendor to the misty gray of the morning.

The regiments went down the hill into the
hollow and across it, splashing into the
swollen creek, crashing through the brush, the
perfect order lost because it could not be
helped … Contrary to expectation, and to my
great delight, the gorge was passed and the
hill-top gained without the firing of a shot.

After carefully crossing Tilghman Creek, Wallace moved his
three brigades into position at the edge of Jones Field and
reformed. While that was in progress, Wallace used field
glasses to look for the enemy, wondering what had become of
him. Wallace was very cautious on this second day of the
battle, and he waited for support from Sherman before moving
against the Confederate line. Sherman crossed Tilghman at
about 10:00 a.m. while Wallace's men were under fire from
one of Ketchum's battery, which had been pushed through
Jones Field, where he set up on its southern edge. Brown was
ordered onto the opposite edge of the field to shell the enemy
in the woods. When he ran out of ammunition, Thurber took
over and the duel continued.

When Sherman joined the 3rd Division, Wallace was able to
move Thurber into the center of the field to duel with Ketchum, and then lead his 1st Brigade against the Confederate
line. Led by the 1st Brigade, Wallace's division moved through
Jones Field but ran into enemy fire in the woods near Sowell
Field. Soon, however, they were able to push through and
advance to Sowell Field. All three brigades then concentrated
their attack against the Confederate's left flank, which was
forced to fall back. Shortly after noon, the division shifted
more to the southwest, forward and right, and moved into
Crescent Field.

For several more hours, a severe struggle raged in the woods and Crescent Field. When additional reinforcements from both McClernand and McCook's division of Buell's Army arrived, the Confederates realized holding their left flank had become hopeless and withdrew to the main Confederate line. Shortly thereafter, the entire Union line was pushing against the rebel line and around 4:00 p.m. Beauregard ordered a complete retreat of his forces. The battle of Shiloh was over.

CHAPTER 10: Halleck's Scapegoat

Nothing like the Battle of Shiloh had ever occurred in the Western Hemisphere. In fact, the two days fighting at Shiloh had produced more casualties than all the previous wars of the United States, combined. Confederate casualties were more than 10,000 killed, wounded or missing, including one of their most capable commanders, while the Union lost over 13,000. Beyond the grisly statistics, Americans north and south of the Mason-Dixon line were suddenly confronted with the sobering fact that Shiloh had not been the decisive battle-to-end-all-battles; there was no crushing victory — only death and carnage on a scale previously unimaginable.

Although Shiloh represented a Union victory, Grant endured severe criticism, especially from the press. This included the accusation that casualties were unnecessarily high due to Grant's lack of preparation. Critics felt Grant should have been entrenched at Pittsburg Landing. Critics cited Grant's absence from the field at the onset of day one which contributed to the initial retreat and chaos on that day. Further widespread criticism led to speculation that Grant had been drinking, which explained his initial absence from the field. A judge from Iowa wrote a blistering attack on Grant in the newspapers: "The criminal carelessness, or something worse, on the part of General Grant, whereby so many brave soldiers were slaughtered."

So intense was the disapproval of Grant after Shiloh, Halleck combined and reorganized his armies, relegating Grant to the powerless position of second-in-command. As learned from an unpublished letter from Halleck to Grant dated May 12, 1862, it is clear Grant was not being punished, rather Halleck was trying to save Grant's career:

You certainly will not suspect me of any intention to injure your feelings or reputation or to do you any injustice; if so, you will eventually change your mind on this subject. For the last three months I have done everything in my power to ward off the attacks which were made upon you. If you believe me your friend you will not require explanations; if not, explanations on my part would be of little avail.

Regardless, Halleck still faced the task of placing the blame of the massive slaughter at Shiloh on someone. That someone would become Lew Wallace. Halleck's actions would actually be twofold: finding a scapegoat for Shiloh and removing two politically appointed generals, USV Lew Wallace and USV John McClernand.

To distract criticism away from Grant, and to make Wallace out to be the cause of the massive death-rate the first day, a running controversy of the battle emerged: disputes over the time Grant issued his order to Wallace, the wording of the order given to Baxter and transmitted by him, the time and manner in which Wallace received it, the time Wallace started his march, the speed and distance of his advance, and the time he received the second and third orders. Grant even insisted that even if Wallace had not been informed of the new positions of the two armies he should have deduced the location of the Union forces from the sound of the guns. The crux of the dispute always included whether Grant, as he claimed, ordered Wallace to march by the road nearest the river, or whether, as Wallace claimed, the order he received instructed him to march to the right of the army. Unfortunately for Wallace, as previously mentioned, one of his officers placed the written order from Baxter under his sword belt, forgot he had put in there, and lost it during the battle.

———

As noted by Otto Eisenschiml in his *The Story of Shiloh* (1946), "The right and the wrong of this controversy has never been definitely established. After carefully sifting the evidence, most students will be inclined to side with Wallace. Grant should have put an order of such paramount importance into writing, instead of letting a staff officer transcribe it at his own discretion. Unfortunately, the tobacco-stained, crumpled piece of paper, written in pencil and unsigned, which carried the directions to Wallace has been lost, and therefore final judgment on this matter must be suspended. Curiously enough, though, if Wallace had been allowed to continue on his march, he would have struck the unprotected left flank of the Confederate army and might have been the instrument to snatch victory from defeat. At half past three in the afternoon, when he was ordered to turn back, he was only a mile from the camps Sherman and McClernand had occupied in the morning. The Confederate army had fought all day long. Its left wing was beginning to celebrate in the abandoned camps and might have stampeded. By recalling Wallace, Grant lost a golden opportunity to pay his opponents back for their surprise attack of the morning, and under conditions which could easily have changed the fortunes of the day."

While this was written in 1946, by and large, it remains the same basic conclusion reached by Charles G. Beemer in his 2015 publication, *My Greatest Quarrel with Fortune: Major General Lew Wallace in the West, 1861-1862*. Also, in her thorough study of Wallace's military career, *Shadow of Shiloh* (2010), Gail Stephens makes a compelling case that Wallace's version of events is the most logical. Timothy B. Smith, a former Park Ranger at the battlefield and a historian who authored *The Untold Story of Shiloh: The Battle and the Battlefield*, agrees.

*   *   *

After taking over the field command from Grant upon arriving on April 12, Halleck was reinforced by both Major-General John Pope and Major-General George Thomas. This then gave him an army of over 120,000 men with whom to assault Beauregard's much smaller force at Corinth. Halleck's main goal, though, was to prevent the movement of Confederate troops into and out of the Mississippi Valley by way of the Memphis and Charleston Railroad at Corinth. True to his West Point training and study of military science, his movement was infuriatingly slow. (He would not capture Corinth until May 30—by then Beauregard was long gone.) Then on April 30, Halleck reorganized his army by pulling McClernand and Wallace out of the front line and creating a new reserve division to guard the army's right and rear. A further insult to Wallace was when McClernand was placed in command.

Following the taking of Corinth, McClernand's reserve division was sent to western Tennessee to secure Union resupply railroad lines, ultimately hoping to capture Memphis. Wallace, however, making clear in a letter to his wife, longed for a bold and energetic pursuit of the Confederates. "Even after participating in the bloodletting at Shiloh, Wallace still saw war as a romantic adventure, full of the promise of glory" (Stephens, 2010). This impatience would cause him to act in such a way as to nearly get him court marshaled.

———

On June 6, in what is now known as First Battle of Memphis, eight rebel vessels opposing nine Union gunboats fought on the Mississippi River immediately above the city of Memphis. Each was armed with only one or two light caliber guns that would be ineffective against the armor of the gunboats. The primary weapon of each was its reinforced prow, which was intended to be used in ramming opponents. The battle, which took less than two hours in the early morning hours, resulted in the immediate surrender of the city of Memphis to Federal authority. However, only two Union regiments were left to control the city.

Following Halleck's desire to keep supply lines open, Wallace was ordered to occupy the railroad east of Memphis. Once securing the rail lines, Wallace proposed moving into Memphis to strengthen Union control. Twice, his requests were rejected—he was to guard the railroad. Later, when rumors of Confederate cavalry patrols in the region arose, Wallace, after being told twice not to, boldly marched into town and took control on June 7. Then the unthinkable happened: a train on the line Wallace was supposed to be patrolling was destroyed, and several members of his division were captured.

Making a triumphant march into Memphis only reinforced Halleck's low opinion of him. "Not only had Wallace disobeyed orders in entering Memphis, he also had failed to guard the railroad" (Stephens, 2010). Wallace's command over the city was short; Grant arrived on June 23 and command passed to him. While in command of Memphis, Wallace had asked for a twenty day leave of absence, which was thereby granted. General Alvin P. Hovey took command of his division, and Wallace left convinced Halleck did not think his service was of any value to the western army.

CHAPTER 11: Cincinnati, Ohio

After being back in Crawfordsville a week, Wallace and Susan traveled to Washington D.C. The purpose of the trip was in part to relieve Susan of her depression she had been recently experiencing and to meet with Secretary of War, Edwin Stanton. Wallace hoped to persuade Stanton to give him a field-command in the eastern theater—freeing him of both Grant and Halleck. Stanton refused his request. Also while there, on July 9, Wallace appeared before the Joint Congressional Committee on the Conduct of War. The committee was interested in investigating General John C. Frémont's declaring martial law throughout The Department of the West (the military affairs in the country west of the Mississippi River to the borders of California and Oregon), the confiscating of property of all those in support of the rebellion, and declaring all slaves, in the area free. The issue at hand was whether Frémont had the authority to make such declarations. The committee, while not charged with such, was also interested in what had happened at Shiloh, news of which was still coming out. In fact, news of Wallace's own failed march had yet to surface. Wallace placed the blame for the first day's high number of casualties and the second day's failure to follow up the attack on Halleck, Grant, and Grant's staff and junior officers. It would not take long for Wallace to realize the damage he inflicted on himself by criticizing Halleck, Grant, and Grant's staff would be irreversible and long lasting.

Concerned with Susan's health, Wallace asked for a second leave, and the Wallaces' traveled up the east coast before returning home. Once back in Crawfordsville, he received a telegram from Governor Morton. On July 2, 1862, President Lincoln called for additional 300,000 three-year volunteers, of which Indiana was expected to supply 31,000. To accomplish this, Morton asked Wallace to tour the state giving speeches. He grudgingly agreed and between July 31 and August 12 spoke in at least six large towns and some smaller ones. Coming to the realization he was never going to get his division back, in August he agreed to take command of the 66th Indiana Volunteers, whose members he had just recruited, but at the rank of colonel. Wallace thereby became part of General Buell's response to the Confederate's invasion of Kentucky.

*   *   *

During the summer of 1862, the Southern General Braxton Bragg headed north and east through Tennessee with an eye on Kentucky. In August 1862, he felt a two-pronged movement, one into the heart of the Bluegrass, and one toward Louisville, should be attempted. He wished to give Kentuckians an opportunity to rally to the Confederate cause and to gain needed supplies. While Kentucky was the immediate goal, ultimately, it was hoped the Ohio River would become the northern boundary of the Confederacy.

To spearhead the march into Central Kentucky, he sent General Edmund Kirby Smith with 12,000 troops, many of them veterans of Shiloh, forward to capture Lexington. General Henry Heth, under Smith's command, with four brigades, fanned north to cover the approaches to Cincinnati. Bragg himself started toward Louisville. Smith moved from the barren, hostile war-torn country of Eastern Tennessee into the heart of Kentucky, the Bluegrass region, rich in supplies. Not until August 29 at Richmond, Kentucky, did he confront 7,000 Union troops of the recently organized Department of the

Ohio, field-commanded by Brigadier-General Mohlon Man-
son. (The Department of the Ohio was organized August 19,
1862, under General Horatio Wright, with headquarters at
Louisville.)

These Union troops were raw recruits from Ohio and Indiana,
with several brigades of loyal Kentuckians and Tennesseans,
and no match against Smith. Consequently, when Smith
attacked on August 30, it led to a humiliating defeat for the
North. The Union loses were 206 killed, 844 wounded, and
4,303 captured or missing. The Confederates lost only 78 men.
This crushing Union defeat at Richmond left the road to the
Ohio River open. Smith then directed General Henry Heth to
march toward the undefended city of Cincinnati. The mounting threat to the nation's sixth largest city and the western
gateway to the North, brought a state of near panic to the civil
and military authorities.

Major-General Horatio Wright, of the Department of the Ohio,
and responsible for Cincinnati's safety, telegraphed Wallace on
September 1 ordering him to assume command of Cincinnati,
along with the sister river cities of Covington and Newport.

Upon arrival, Wallace immediately proclaimed martial law,
suspended business in the cities, and ordered all able-bodied
men to report for duty in the trenches he planned to dig on the
hills beyond Covington and Newport.

The force Wallace was to command when he arrived consisted
of only three companies of regulars in Cincinnati. Several
infantry regiments at Camp Dennison, about fifteen miles
northeast of the city, were hurried to the defense. The 45th and
99th Ohio Infantry Regiments, guarding the southern approach
route along the Licking River in northern Kentucky, fell back

slowly before Heth's advance and eventually joined the defense. Most men in militia organizations in existence in the city before the war were now a part of the regular army away at various fronts.

On the same day the town was placed under martial law, Ohio Governor Tod ordered Ohio's adjutant-general to send any available troops other than those guarding Ohio's southern border to Cincinnati. Tod also ordered the state quartermaster to send five thousand weapons to equip Cincinnati's militia. "To the loyal people of the River Counties," he asked that all loyal men form themselves into companies and regiments to beat back the enemy. The response to the call to arms was remarkable; within 48 hours, civilians from sixty-five counties numbering 15,766 men reported for duty at Cincinnati.

*   *   *

On Wednesday, September 4, General Wright came to Cincinnati and met with Wallace. They planned to defend the city from the hills south of Covington and Newport, Kentucky, where rifle pits and breastworks would be dug. The Ohio River half encircled Newport and Covington, and 16 gunboats would patrol the Ohio above and below. Out on the Lexington Pike (Dixie Highway) crowning the long hill beyond Covington, stood a half-finished fort started by General O. M. Mitchel in June 1862 and named after him. Wallace chose this spot as a starting point and instructed civil engineers to lay out defense lines. The defense lines would stretch from Bromley, Kentucky, on the banks of the Ohio, southwest of Cincinnati, eastward to a spot on the Kentucky shore not far from the mouth of the Little Miami River.

Five days after the proclamation of martial law, the morning reports showed 72,000 men were present. Of these, fully 60,000 were "irregulars." They came into the city armed with pistols, shot-guns, and sporting rifles. On the September 5, Wallace administered the oath of allegiance, and those men without rifles were issued old Springfields.

On both September 4 and 5, ferry boats transported 5,000 men across the river with plows, picks, and shovels to begin work building forts, batteries, and the defense lines. Wallace also had a telegraph line set up the whole length of the works, with stations at every regimental and brigade headquarters. However, Wallace was disturbed at the length of time it took to ferry troops across the river. No bridges existed at the time. Wallace consulted with Cincinnati architect Wesley Cameron regarding the feasibility of placing a pontoon bridge across the Ohio River. Cameron immediately fashioned a bridge that was made of empty coal barges lashed side-by-side and anchored securely to both shores. In the space of two days, Cameron had the pontoon bridge in place.

Pontoon bridge at Cincinnati, Ohio on September 13, 1862

By September 8, preparations for defense of Cincinnati were complete. While, the threat to the city itself was no longer as great, peril to the area still existed. Martial law was lifted, and limited business was resumed. While confidence in Cincinnati's ability to defend itself ran high, newspapers reminded citizens the enemy was only a few miles from Fort Mitchel. Heth bivouacked the majority of his force at Florence, eight miles southwest of Covington, and sent advanced parties to reconnoiter the Union position. These scouts penetrated as far as the outer works of Fort Mitchel, where they skirmished with Wallace's pickets on September 10.

Most of Cincinnati, including Wallace, expected a Confederate attack on the morning of September 11. The troops along the line were ordered to sleep on their arms and to be formed up for battle by three in the morning. River gunboats were warned to be in position to support such a movement. However, after reconnoitering the defenses at various points, the rebels determined an attack would be pointless. Under orders from Kirby Smith, Heth withdrew his force on the night of September 11, thus ending the Siege of Cincinnati.

For a short time, Wallace basked in the national spotlight for his role in defending Cincinnati. The eastern press lauded his "vigorous proclamations," and gave him credit for saving the strategic western city. Cincinnati's *Democratic Enquirer* described Wallace as a "gallant and go ahead young General." The city's *Commercial* reported the citizens were reassured by the general who was "ever alert, faithful and resolute."

The defense of Cincinnati was one of the great accomplishments of Wallace's Civil War career. While Wallace's inspired command "saved Cincinnati," it did little to relieve him of his "shelved" status. As the summer ended, he realized the men with the ability to advance his career had other plans for him.

*   *   *

View North down the main street of Camp Chase, Columbus, Ohio.
The National Archives

On September 17, Wallace was ordered to Columbus, Ohio, to organize paroled Union prisoners at Camp Chase. Parole camps were places where Union soldiers who were Confederate prisoners of War were returned north under Union supervision in a non-combat role. When Wallace arrived, he found less than 3,000 men, as 2,000 had deserted. Many men had no shoes, socks, or pants. Many had not been paid for over a year. After organizing and paying the troops, he was to prepare them to fight an uprising of Sioux Indians in

Minnesota. Accordingly, he organized prisoners into regiments of infantry, cavalry, and artillery and transferred the men to another facility. However, by mid-October, General Pope informed Halleck the Sioux had been defeated. Having carried out his required duties, Wallace ask to be given a field-command suitable to his rank.

Again, to his dismay, in November, Wallace was appointed President of the Buell Commission to investigate Union General Don Carlos Buell's conduct in Kentucky during the summer. The Commission, which met in Cincinnati, Louisville, and Nashville, occupied Wallace's time until May 1863. The Commission found Buell had not been disloyal and was following government policy.

Beginning in December 1863, members of both houses of Congress, led by Senator Henry S. Lane, Wallace's brother-in-law, newspaper editors, even church leaders, began putting pressure on Lincoln, his cabinet, and military leaders encouraging them to give Wallace a command deserving of his rank. All were ignored. As a result, Wallace missed all of the major battles of 1863, including Gettysburg, Chancellorsville, the Chattanooga Campaign, etc. Finally, Wallace's "long wait" ended on March 12, 1864 when he received orders from the War Department to report to Baltimore and to assume command of the VIII Corps and the Middle Department, which included Delaware and Maryland west to the Monocacy River.

The assignment was not a glamorous one. Many of the men assigned to VIII Corps were raw recruits, garrison troops, unseasoned militia and convalescents. Since many of Maryland's citizens sympathized with the rebel cause, Maryland had been placed under martial law. Wallace was forced to spend considerable time and effort suppressing secessionist activities. While carrying out his duties in the Middle Department with great success, Wallace was frustrated by the lack of action. He lamented that "Great battles are to be scented not far off; soon will be heard the thunder of the captains, the sound of the trumpet, and the shouting, and I not there." Yet within a short period of time, Wallace's desire for action would be granted.

CHAPTER 12: Monocacy, Maryland

By July 1864, General Robert E. Lee's Army of Northern Virginia had been driven back to Petersburg, only 25 miles from the Confederate capital at Richmond. Petersburg was a vital railroad hub for the Confederacy. Lee was surrounded by hardened Union forces that outnumbered him two to one under the command of Ulysses S. Grant. Bolstering the Federal ranks were troops from Washington D.C. who had previously manned forts surrounding the city. Their removal left the capital virtually defenseless.

To pull troops away from Petersburg, Lee ordered General Jubal Early to first secure the Shenandoah Valley, and if events permitted, cross the Potomac River and threaten or capture Washington from the north. Once Early forced Union General David Hunter away from Lynchburg, Virginia on June 18, a city that provided crucial railroad ties from southwest Virginia back towards the center of the state, he headed north. Hunter's retreat paved the way for Early to move virtually unopposed through the Shenandoah Valley, into Maryland, and on to Washington. Even though the Confederates were unopposed, their movement was by no means secret. In fact, the president of the Baltimore & Ohio Railroad (B&O), John W. Garrett, used his workforce of railroad agents and engineers to keep tabs on Southern troop movements. Garrett was a strong Unionist, whose goal was to keep B&O tracts connecting Washington, Baltimore, and surrounding areas open. On June 29, he telegraphed Halleck, "Breckinridge and [Early] are reported moving up. I am satisfied the operations and designs of the enemy demand the greatest vigilance and attention."

Similar to Grant's inability to believe the rebels would attack him at Shiloh, Grant refused to believe the Confederates were moving north. Grant said he saw no evidence "which indicated an intention on the part of the rebels to attempt any northern movement." Unaware of Hunter's fate, Grant insisted, "If Genl Hunter is in striking distance, there ought to be veteran forces enough to meet anything the enemy might have." Even Assistant Secretary of War Charles Dana reported on July 5 there "seemed to [be] pretty good evidence that Early was with Lee defending Petersburg." Consequently, on the July 8, Early and some 15,000 troops were on the outskirts of Frederick, Maryland.

The town of Frederick sat at the crossroads of several key highway and rail routes. The Georgetown Pike to Washington, the National Road to Baltimore, and the B&O Railroad all converged here. Just south of Frederick runs the Monocacy River, a tributary of the Potomac. Running north to south, its name comes from the Shawnee language for "river of many bends." At that time, it had steep banks and was much deeper than it is now. It could only be crossed by bridge or at one of several fording sites.

In addition to informing Washington of Early's movement, on July 3 Garrett also carried the alarm to Middle Department of Maryland and Delaware commanded by General Lew Wallace. He told Wallace he had reports from his agents that Confederate troops were engaging in serious operations in the Shenandoah Valley. He also expressed serious concerns that rebel forces would attack Washington. Thus, he suggested to Wallace, whose jurisdiction extended only to the Monocacy

River, to send troops there to stop the Confederate advance. Upon hearing this news, Wallace reasoned, if the rebels were indeed crossing into Maryland, this meant they were unusually reckless or strong enough to seriously face opposition. If they were strong, then they might be contemplating an attack on Washington. Reinforcing this thought was the fact most of the Union forces that had once been stationed there had been pulled south to Petersburg. In the event they should reach Washington, in all likelihood they would destroy the Navy Yard, negotiable bonds and currency, six-acres of supplies for the Army of the Potomac, 32,000 horses and 15,000 mules, munition depots, and medical depots.

True to his word, on a train provided by Garrett, Wallace and aide, Colonel James Ross, arrived at Monocacy early in the morning of July 6. The seriousness of his mission took on reality when he received word that a column of rebel cavalry had been spotted in the Middletown Valley, ten miles west of Frederick, moving eastward; meaning, the Confederate's goal was not Pennsylvania (as with Gettysburg), but Washington, Baltimore, or the Maryland Heights—but which of the three? In addition to determining Early's objective, Wallace sought to slow Early's advance so to give Grant time to send a corps north, determine Early's full strength, and keep a line of retreat open. In light of these objectives, Wallace chose the east bank of the Monocacy River to make his stand.

While Wallace stayed in Baltimore, the day after Garrett's visit, he began ordering troops to the river under the command of General Erastus Tyler. Tyler's first order from Wallace was to deploy Wallace's own First Separate Brigade. Tyler then mobilized five companies of the First Potomac Home Brigade, part of the 3rd Potomac Home Brigade, the 12th Maryland Infantry Regiment, three companies of the 144th Ohio Infantry

Regiment and seven of the 149th Ohio Infantry Regiment. The force also included the six three-inch rifled guns of the Baltimore Battery of Light Artillery and one 24-pounder howitzer. The cavalry at Wallace's disposal consisted of 250 men of the 8th Illinois Calvary, some 100 men of the 159th Ohio National Guard, 250 horsemen from several units in the area, and the Loudoun Rangers—a loosely organized cavalry troop. In total, Wallace had at his disposal about 3,200 men, most of whom were "hundred days men" (enlistments of three months) who served as temporary garrison troops and had never seen battle.

At last, by July 5, Halleck came to the realization Early's move was an "invasion" and one "of a pretty formidable character." This realization spurred Halleck and Grant, as Lee had hoped, to send significant numbers of troops north. On July 6, two brigades of the Union army's Sixth Corps' Third Division, some 4,000 men, under the command of General James Ricketts, left their encampment outside Petersburg, Virginia. Their original assignment was to go to Harpers Ferry, but when the division reached Monocacy Junction, Wallace explained the pending crisis and they decided to join the defense. Because the division arrived so late on July 8, the next morning Early was still under the impression he was facing only "hundred days men".

The "junction" part of the battle name refers to the B&O railroad switching junction built on the west side of the river. Here, the track was laid in a triangle with switches at each point. By backing up and switching tracks, a locomotive could change directions or turn around without a roundhouse. The junction itself was not an objective in this battle; however, it saw some of the heaviest fighting.

Monocacy Junction as it appeared during the war.
National Parks Service

*　　　*　　　*

On the day of the battle, Wallace had three bridges to defend. the Stone (Jug) Bridge, which carried the Baltimore Pike (National Road), and two bridges at Monocacy Junction—the railroad bridge and the wooden Georgetown Pike bridge a few hundred yards downstream.

Wallace:

Early in the morning of the 9th [preparations] for battle [were] made.

The right, forming an extended line from the railroad, was given General Tyler, who, by direction, had left Colonel Brown at the stone bridge on the Baltimore pike with his command, and the company of mounted infantry. Upon the holding of that bridge depended the security of my right flank, and the line of retreat to Baltimore.

Three companies … were posted to defend Crum's Ford-midway the stone bridge and railroad …

The battery was divided-Ricketts and Tyler each received three guns.

On the left, as it was likely to be the main point of attack, I directed General Ricketts to form his command in two lines across the Georgetown pike, so as to hold the rising ground south of it and the wooden bridge across the river.

Still farther to the left, Colonel Clendenin took post to watch that flank and guard the lower fords …

On the western bank of the river, Captain Brown's detachment of the First Regiment Potomac Home Brigade was deployed as skir-mishers, in a line three quarters of a mile to the front.

24-pounder howitzer   Blockhouse

A 24-pounder howitzer was left in a rude
earthwork near the block-house by the railroad, where it could be used to defend the two
bridges and cover the retirement and crossing
of the skirmishers.

*   *   *

On July 9, General Early rode out of the southeastern limits of
Frederick and found himself on a vast plain which stretched
about two and a half miles eastward to the Monocacy River.
Beyond the river lay green cornfields, open ground from a
small distance, and then a range of hills which blocked Baltimore and partially screened Washington. Two main roads
diverged in an opening angle from the river: the Georgetown
Pike running to his right, the Baltimore Pike to his left. The
B&O tracks ran eastward along the Georgetown Pike.

*   *   *

Wallace:

While our slender breakfast was getting ready
in the morning, I walked out to the bluff by
the railroad bridge. Everywhere I read the
promise of a beautiful summer day. There was
not a speck in the sky, and the departing
night had left a coolness in the air delicious
and most refreshing. Behind me little columns
of smoke were slowly rising; the same
indications across the river told where our
pickets were in post and wide awake; beyond
them, in the direction of Frederick, a denser
smoke lay along the earth in the form of a
pallid cloud hanging not higher than a tree-
top, and it spoke of the enemy; and everywhere
friends and foes alike were at coffee or
making it. The smell of new mown hay from the
yellowing stubble-fields was lost in the sooty
perfume of the many fires.

Breakfast over, with my staff I rode to
General Ricketts, and found him down in the
low land of the little creek not far from the
mill, and together we went to get a look at
his men in position. With my glass I swept the
country in the direction of the city, search-
ing for signs of the enemy. Directly I caught
sight of a dark line beginning to stretch
itself out on the Buckeystown road.

"They are moving," I said to Ricketts.

"Which way?"

"This way," I answered, and passed the glass to him.

In a few seconds he gave me the glass back, saying:

"Two miles and more. We can reach them easily."

Turning to one of his officers. "Ride," he said, "and tell Captain — What is his name?"

"Alexander," I returned.

"Tell Captain Alexander to open fire." Then to me,

"There's something in having the first shot."

*   *   *

Late on the evening of July 8, General Taylor ordered Colonel Brown, commander of the 149th Ohio National Guard, to protect the Stone (Jog) Bridge on the Baltimore Pike along with the 144th Ohio National Guard. At daylight, the 149th Ohio established a skirmish line on the west side of the

Monocracy River. Confederate sharpshooters from General Robert Rhodes' division engaged Brown's Ohioans.

Rhodes' objective was to attack the Stone Bridge and draw as many Union troops from Monocracy Junction as possible. The Confederates surprised the outnumbered Union left flank, using terrain to hide their movement, and force the Union defenders back to within one hundred yards of the bridge. Brown ordered two counter attacks; the second one successfully drove the Confederates back. In the course of the day, "The enemy seemed to have stopped pursuit at the stone bridge (General Lew Wallace's Report on the Battle of Monocacy, 2016).

———

To protect the attack on the two bridges at Monocacy Junction, Wallace counted on the artillery: the 24-pounder Howitzer, and Captain Frederick Alexander's guns. Once these weapons were well-placed, Lieutenant George Davis and 75 men of the 10th Vermont crossed the covered bridge and reported to Captain Brown near the blockhouse. Their orders were "to hold the bridges at all hazards." In addition to the 75 Vermonters and Brown's 200 1st Regiment Potomac Home Brigade, there were about 25 pickets from the 9th New York Heavy Artillery (Bearss, 2003). Lieutenant Abbot of the 10th Vermont noted, the skirmish line "crescent shaped with the convex side ... toward Frederick with its flanks resting practically on the river." Due to misidentifying Confederates as Federal soldiers, leading to the death of numerous Union men, Brown turned command over to Lieutenant George Davis.

Between 9 and 10 a.m., Confederate General Ramseur moved south along the Georgetown Pike and began skirmishing with

Union pickets near the bridges. This attack on the junction failed due to the Union's strong position. The two sides then settled down to artillery and sharpshooter exchanges. A second attack on the junction was launched around 11:00 a.m. and quickly became fierce. In describing the fighting, Confederate Captain Turners recalls, "[We were] ordered to capture the blockhouse on the other side of the Baltimore & Ohio railroad. A considerable force of the enemy was in a railroad cut [tracks]and perfectly protected ... [and we] were met by a hot enfilading fire ... and the regiment was driven back." Confederate Colonel Blacknall later wrote, "We performed the task of driving the Union skirmish line splendidly ... driving the enemy back to their fortifications on the railroad, where they took refuge in a blockhouse constructed of heavy timbers ... I then charged them in this position coming within 20 feet of the house in which they were posted but finding it impossible to carry it by storm, we fell back." After the Union's stiff resistance, Ramseur concluded that to cross the river at the Georgetown Pike would be too costly. Early agreed, "The enemy's position was too strong and the difficulties of crossing the Monocacy under fire too great." A flanking movement seemed the only alternative. Even though the battle would shift to Wallace's left flank, he decided it best to burn both the Georgetown bridge and the blockhouse.

At that moment, Early showed his hand. It was Washington he was after, not Baltimore, or the Maryland Heights, so he needed to get control of the Georgetown Pike as quickly as possible—he must reach Washington before Grant's veterans arrived. Therefore, if Wallace's left were smashed, the George-town Pike would be open to the rebels.

General Early decided to send columns to his own right, but he first had to find a ford large enough for his men to cross. In the meantime, Confederate sharpshooters were put in the Best barn to pick away at the Federals. As more Confederate artillery were brought forward, Union gunners returned fire and set the barn aflame. Suddenly, a line of rebel cavalry cantered into view on Early's right, splashed across the Monocacy at Worthington Ford, about a mile below the wooden bridge. They were members of John McCausland's Cavalry Brigade coming in from a railroad and telegraph cutting expedition between Harpers Ferry and Washington. Once across the river, the troopers quickly dismounted and readied to move forward.

In their battle line, McCausland's men set off down a hill and towards the Federal left. When Wallace noted this, he ordered Ricketts to change his front to that direction and advance to a field of waist-high corn, divided by a fence running between the C.K. Thomas and Worthington farms. Upon reaching the fence, they were to conceal themselves out of view of the advancing Confederates. Sensing no opposition, the rebels advanced "with banners and guidons waving" to within 125 yards of the Union line. At that moment, the whole Federal line of infantry rose to its feet, rested their guns on the upper rails of the fence, took aim and fired. Years later, as an adult, Glenn Worthington recalled watching from the basement window "how the whole rebel line disappeared as if swallowed up in the earth" (see Quint, 2016).

Quickly regrouping, McCausland's men slipped around the left of Rickett's advance line and attacked again, seizing the house and outbuildings of the Thomas farm. From this new position, the Confederates were sheltered and high enough to turn the fight, according to Wallace, "red-hot." When the rebels wavered, Wallace ordered Ricketts to charge and dislodge them. As Wallace hoped, the Confederates retreated, accompanied by shouting and cheering from his staff.

The third and final attack by the Confederates on the left of the Union line began at 3:30 p.m. General John B. Gordon led three brigades of infantry under Generals William Terry, Zebulon York, and Clement Evens back across the Worthington and Thomas farms. The southern troops marched right into Rickett's division of battle-hardened troops. What ensued was a vicious, full-bore field battle that turned the tide of the Battle of Monocacy in the Confederate's favor.

Gordon had about 3,600 fresh men and decided to attack *en echelon*—hoping to deliver a one-two-three punch against Rickett's division. Aiding Gorgon was Early's artillery firing from both sides of the river on the Union's rear and flank. Rickett had about 3,300 men, but they had been engaged much of the afternoon.

Evan's Georgia Brigade made the first attack, but was stymied by the stiff Union response. York's two brigades from Louisiana pushed the Union left and center back to the Georgetown Pike, an old sunken road. However, their attack was also checked due to the strong Union position in the natural-made trench. Finally, Terry's brigade charged right of the Union line which somehow held despite earlier having men rushed from the right to reinforce the left—leaving only one full regiment—and losing artillery support due to shortage of ammunition. Rickett's men tried to regain the hill earlier lost but were rebuffed due to Confederate artillery fire from across the river. Then Gordon found the key to victory. He ordered Terry's brigade to move along the riverbed below the bottom of the hill out of the Federal's sight. When they moved out of cover onto the hill, they were on the Union's right flank firing down into the Georgetown Pike. The Union defense crumbled, retreated, and because the Confederates were not only hammering Rickett's front, but also his flank, the Union soldiers were fighting for their lives.

*   *   *

With Wallace's retreat to Baltimore, the road lay open to Washington. On July 10 the Confederates began the march toward the Union capital. By midday on Monday July 11, Early arrived at Fort Stevens, where he could see the dome of the U.S. Capitol through his glasses. With his troops straggling behind him, exhausted from the heat and the long march, Early decided to delay the attack on the fort until July 12. Although artillery exchanges and skirmishes occurred on July 11, prior to the full-scale attack, Early was too late. The Union VI Corps Grant had dispatched to Washington, had already arrived and were prepared to defend the city. The Confederate infantry, reduced to 8,000 men, was unable to continue, and by July 14 Early had crossed the Potomac at White's Ferry into Virginia.

The final Federal casualty figures were 98 killed, 594 wounded, and 1188 captured or missing, for a total of 1880. Early estimated his losses at Monocacy and in his attacks on the Washington defenses as between 600 and 700.

In writing about the Battle of Monocacy in his official report, Wallace said, "These men died to save the National Capital and they did save it."

And for Wallace, the battle meant exoneration.

CONCLUSION

As a young man, Wallace showed a knack for recruiting, organizing, and drilling militias. In acquiring a copy of General Winfield Scott's *Infantry Tactics: Or, Rules for the Exercise and Maneuvers of the United States' Infantry,* Wallace gained knowledge about the art of war far above those of his fellow volunteer generals, as well as many West Point graduates. As a military man, Wallace competently demonstrated his abilities.

At Romney, he had exhibited a keen appreciation for spontaneous thinking and action. At Donelson, he displayed independent thinking and audacity, seizing the initiative. At Shiloh, on April 7, he once again led men in battle successfully. At Cincinnati, he revealed a superb skill for defensive organization. At Monocacy, when others refused to listen to and analyze what little intelligence they had, Wallace moved rapidly, showing an uncanny knack for getting the job done, despite the odds (Beemer, 2015).

Wallace's military service ended with his involvement in two of the war's most notorious events. First, he served on the military commission that tried the Lincoln conspirators, and second, as president of the military court that tried Captain Henry Wirz. Wirz was the commander of the Confederate prisoner-of-war camp at Andersonville, Georgia.

After the war, Wallace returned to Indiana in 1867 to practice law, and made two unsuccessful bids for a seat in Congress (in 1868 and 1870). As a reward for his political support for the Republican presidential candidate Rutherford B. Hayes in the

1876 election, he was appointed governor of the New Mexico Territory, where he served from August 1878 to March 1881. His next assignment came in March 1881, when Republican President James A. Garfield appointed Wallace to an overseas diplomatic post in Constantinople, Turkey, as U.S. Minister to the Ottoman Empire. Wallace remained in this post until 1885. In the 1880s, he wrote the bestselling novel *Ben-Hur: A Tale of the Christ*. Wallace died February 15, 1905 and is buried in Oak Hill Cemetery in Crawfordsville, Indiana.

*   *   *

General Lew Wallace
Statuary Hall in the U.S. Capitol
(Photo by Matt Elmstedt, 2010)

General Wallace had a natural aptitude for the field; he possessed all the qualities for successful military leadership. He was methodical, aggressive, courageous, and discreet. He appreciated the value of discipline and all things that made for the comfort and efficiency of his command. He possessed the rare quality of being able to attract and hold the confidence and affection of his army.

From the February 26, 1910 address by Congressman Edgar D. Crumpacker of Indiana during the PROCEEDINGS IN THE HOUSE accepting from the State of Indiana the statue of General Lew Wallace, erected in Statuary Hall in the U.S. Capitol.

SOURCES

YouTube
- Battle of Monocacy Fiber Optic Exhibit
- Lew Wallace, WTIU
- Destination Frederick County: Monocacy National Battlefield
- Gail Stephens: The Battle of Shiloh
- Shiloh Fiery Trail HD
- USMEXICAN_WAR01
- The Battle of Monocacy: The Fight that Saved Washington D.C.

C-Span
- Union General Lew Wallace's Monocacy Defense Ryan Quint
- Desperate Engagement: Battlefield Tour Marc Leepson

*   *   *

Beemer, Charles G.
My Greatest Quarrel with Fortune: Major General Lew Wallace in the West, 1861-1862
The Kent State University Press
2015
ISBN-13: 978-1606352366

Boomhower,Ray E.
The Sword & the Pen: A Life of Lew Wallace
Indiana Historical Society
2005
ISBN-13: 978-0871951854

Carrington, General Henry B.
"Major general Lew Wallace at Shiloh"
The Bay State Monthly Volume II John N. McClintock and
Company, 1885

Cashon, John Philip
Paducah and the Civil War
History Press Library Editions
2016
ISBN-13: 978-1540200525

Catton, Bruce
Grant Moves South
Little Brown & Co. 1960
2000
ISBN-13: 978-0785812647

_____. *Terrible Swift Sword* Volume 2 (American Civil War
Trilogy)
Phoenix Press
1988
ISBN-13: 978-1898800248

Century Co,
The Leaders Of The Civil War Volume I Part Ii
Publication date 1884
P. 534-5

Daniel, Larry J.
Shiloh: The Battle That Changed the Civil War
Simon & Schuster
1998
ISBN-13: 978-0684838571

Eisenschiml, Otto
The story of Shiloh
Civil War Round Table, Chicago
1946
Chicago, Norman Press

French, Wm. H.
Instruction for Field Artillery
(The 1864 field artillery tactics)
United States. Army. Field Artillery, United States. Army
J. B. LIPPINCOTT & CO.
1861
Scholarly Publishing Office, University of Michigan Library
(December 22, 2005)
Language: English
ISBN-13: 978-1425560911

Geaslen, Chester F
Our moment of glory in the Civil War: When Cincinnati, "The Queen City of the West" and sixth largest city was defended from the hills of northern Kentucky
Otto Printing Co
1972

Goss, Thomas Joseph
The War Within the Union High Command: Politics and Generalship during the Civil War
University Press of Kansas
2003
ISBN-13: 978-0700612635

"Address of Mr. Crumpacker of Indiana"
Proceedings in Statuary Hall and The Senate and The House of Representatives upon the Unveiling, Reception, and Acceptance from The State of Indiana of The Statue of General Lew Wallace
Washington, Government Printing Office
1910

Kunkel, Jack
The Battle of Shiloh: A Step by Step Account of One of the Greatest Battles of the Civil War
Pepper Publishing
2013
Sold by: Amazon Digital Services LLC
ASIN: B00B2P2X02

Leepson, Marc
Desperate Engagement: How a Little-Known Civil War Battle Saved Washington, D.C., and Changed American History
Thomas Dunne Books
2007
ISBN-13: 978-0312363642

Lossing, Benson John
Pictorial History of the Civil War in the United States of America, Volume 2
1866
Philadelphia, G. W. Childs

McKee, Irving
Ben-Hur Wallace: The Life of General Lew Wallace
University of California Press
1947

Monocacy National Battlefield Staff
The Battle of Monocacy - July 9, 1864
Western Maryland Interpretive Association
2010
ISBN: 9780984570706

Morsberger, Robert E., and Katharine M. Morsberger.
Lew Wallace, militant romantic
San Francisco Book Co
1980
ISBN-13: 978-0070433052

Paarlberg, Larry, Gobel, Erin, McGuire, Amanda
Courage and Conflict: Lew Wallace in 1862
General Lew Wallace Study & Museum
2015
Sold by: Amazon Digital Services LLC
ASIN: B00XRU42JK

_____. *Trials and Tribulations: Lew Wallace in 1865*
General Lew Wallace Study & Museum
2015
Sold by: Amazon Digital Services LLC
ASIN: B00XRWGMN2

_____. *Vindication: Lew Wallace in 1864*
Cain, Stephanie, Paarlberg, Larry, McGuire, Amanda
General Lew Wallace Study & Museum
2015
Sold by: Amazon Digital Services LLC
ASIN: B00XRU3Z3O

Quint, Ryan
Determined to Stand and Fight: The Battle of Monocacy, July 9, 1864
Savas Beatie
2017
ISBN-13: 978-1611213461

Stephens, Gail
Shadow of Shiloh: Major General Lew Wallace in the Civil War
Indiana Historical Society
2010
ISBN-13: 978-0871952875

_____. *Embattled: General Lew Wallace's Leadership in the Civil War*
General Lew Wallace Study & Museum
2015
Sold by: Amazon Digital Services LLC
ASIN: B00XRQ2KVQ

Stewart, Richard W., General Editor
American Military History, volume 1: the United States Army and the Forging of a Nation, 1775-1917
Center of Military History United States Army
2004
ISBN 0-16-072362-0

United States. War Dept
Instruction for field artillery
1861
PHILADELPHIA:
J. B. LIPPINCOTT & CO.

Vandiver, Frank
Jubal's Raid: General Early's Famous Attack on Washington in 1864
University of Nebraska Press; Reprint edition
1992
ISBN-13: 978-0803296107

Wallace, Lew
An Autobiography, Vol. 1
Forgotten Books
2012
ASIN: B008K99F6S

_____. *An Autobiography Vol. 2*
Forgotten Books
2017
ISBN-13: 978-1331980537

_____. *Smoke, Sound and Fury: The Civil War Memoirs of Major-General Lew* Wallace, U.S. Volunteers
ED: Jim Leeke
Strawberry Hill Press
1998
ISBN-13: 978-0894071355

_____"My Own Account of the First Day at Shiloh".
Appleton's Booklovers Magazine, vol. vii. January-June, 1906, p. 72. Copyright. 1905. 1906, by D. Appleton and Company

Woodworth, Steven E.
The Shiloh Campaign
Southern Illinois University Press
2009
ISBN-13: 978-0809328925

*   *   *

Buley, R. C. "Indiana In The Mexican War." Indiana Magazine of History 15, no. 3 (1919): 260-92.
jstor.org/stable/27785913.

Burks, Peter B.
"Major-General Lew Wallace: His Military Career"
Paper present for partial fulfillment Bachelor of Arts degree
Hanover College
1971

Elwood, John R.
"Dennis Hart Mahan (1802-1871) and his influence on West Point"
West Point, Tactical Officer Education Program
1995

Gray, David O
"Lew Wallace at Shiloh: Goat or Scapegoat"
Graduate thesis
American Public University System
Charles Town, West Virginia
2014

Haselberger, Fritz
"Wallace's Raid on Romney in 1861"
West Virginia History 27, no. 2
(January 1966)

Mortenson,Christopher Ryan
"Lew Wallace and the Civil War: Politics and Generalship "
Ph.D. Dissertation
Texas A&M University
2007

Rean Daniel T., CWO3 USN
"Shifting Strategies: Military Theory in the American Civil War
"

MilitaryHistoryOnline.com
2008

Somers, Lucas R
"Major General Lew Wallace at Shiloh"
The Student Researcher: A Phi Alpha Theta Publication
History Student Publications
Western Kentucky University
2014

Stern, Joseph S., Jr
"The Siege of Cincinnati"
Bulletin of the Historical and Philosophical Society of Ohio,
Vol. 18, No. 3. July 1960, pages 162-186.

"Panic on the Ohio! Confederate Advance on Cincinnati, September 1862"
    Introduction, by Geoffrey R. Walden
    Panic in Cincinnati, by James A. Ramage
    The Defenses of Cincinnati, by Geoffrey R. Walden
Blue & Gray Magazine
Volume III, 1985-86
www.cincinnaticwrt.org/data/panic.html

VOLPE, Vernon L.
"Dispute Every Inch of Ground": Major General Lew Wallace Commands Cincinnati, September 1862. Indiana Magazine of History
June 1989.
ISSN 1942-9711

*   *   *

Internet
Mexican American War and the Treaty of Guadalupe-Hidalgo
https://www.nps.gov/cham/learn/historyculture/mexican-american-war.htm

Mexican American War History
http://www.thomaslegion.net/mexicanwar.html

The Annexation of Texas, the Mexican American War, and the Treaty of Guadalupe-Hidalgo, 1845–1848
https://history.state.gov/milestones/1830-1860/texas-annexation

The Battle for Stone (Jug) Bridge
BATTLE OF MONOCACY
https://southmountaincw.wordpress.com/category/battle-of-monocacy/

The Battle of Monocacy Summary & Facts
https://www.civilwar.org/learn/civil-war/battles/monocacy

The Battle of Monocacy, 9 July 1864
https://armyhistory.org/the-battle-of-monocacy-9-july-1864/

Monocacy: National Park Service
https://www.nps.gov/mono/index.htm

Battle of Monocacy Junction
http://www.exploringoffthebeatenpath.com/Battlefields/Mon
ocacy/index.html

Ryan Quint and the Monocacy 150th
    Part I: A General Fallen from Grace: Lew Wallace before
    Monocacy
    Part II: A General Redeemed: Lew Wallace and the Battle
    of Monocacy
    Part III: A General Remembered: Lew Wallace after the
    Battle of Monocacy
    https://emergingcivilwar.com/2014/07/09/ryan-quint-
    and-the-monocacy-150th/

Civil War Series, The Battle of Shiloh NPS
https://www.nps.gov/parkhistory/online_books/civil_war_se
ries/22/sec1.htm

Lincoln Parade Transparency, 1860
http://americanhistory.si.edu/collections/search/object/nma
h_513759

The Falls of the Ohio
https://artistatexit0.wordpress.com/2010/09/21/the-
waterfalls/

Defense of Cincinnati, September 1 - 20, 1862
https://civilwaref.blogspot.com/2013/09/defense-of-
cincinnati-september-1-13.html

TROUBLE AT PADUCAH
https://www.nytimes.com/1861/12/08/archives/trouble-at-
paducah.html

Shiloh: Place of Peace to Bloody Battlefield (A Lesson Plan)
NPS
**www.nps.gov/teachers/classrooms/shiloh-
battlefield-teacher-packet.htm#**

General Lew Wallace's Report on the Battle of Monocacy
https://ironbrigader.com/2016/07/09/general-lew-wallaces-
report-battle-monocacy/

David B. McCoy earned his history teaching degree from Ashland University and his graduate degree from Kent State University. After teaching thirty-two years, David retired to write short books on a wide variety of topics. He also holds certificates of completion from FEMA and the Columbia Regional Learning Center for personal emergency prepared-ness. Recently he received a certificate of completion in "COVOD-19: What You Need to Know" from the Interstate Postgraduate Medical Association.

Short, concise, and informative, most of his publications are less than 100 pages. Ebooks are around $4.99 with print copies costing a few dollars more. Books are available only from Amazon.

Royalties are donated to nonprofit organizations.

https://sparechangepress.weebly.com

amazon.com/author/davidmccoy

Made in the USA
Middletown, DE
20 August 2021

46385551R00078